HIGH PLAINS

PRESS

Soap Suds Row

Artwork from National Park Service, San Juan Island National Historic Park.

Soap Suds Row

THE BOLD LIVES OF
ARMY LAUNDRESSES, 1802–1876

Jennie Lawrence

Jennifer J. Lawrence

HIGH PLAINS PRESS

Front Cover illustration: *When the Guns Fell Silent* © L. D. Edgar
For information or prints contact: www.WesternHeritageStudio.com

LIBRARY OF CONGRESS CATALOGING-IN-PUBLICATION DATA

Names: Lawrence, Jennifer J., author.
Title: Soap suds row : the bold lives of Army laundresses, 1802-1876 / Jennifer J. Lawrence.
Other titles: Bold lives of Army laundresses, 1802-1876
Description: Glendo, WY : High Plains Press, [2016] | Includes bibliographical references and index.
Identifiers: LCCN 2016003856 | 9781937147099 (hardcover : alk. paper) | ISBN 9781937147105 (pbk. : alk. paper)
Subjects: LCSH: United States. Army--Women--History--19th century. | United States. Army--Women--History--19th century. | United States. Army--Women--Biography. | United States. Army--Military life--History--19th century. | Laundresses--United States--History--19th century. | Laundresses--United States--Social conditions--19th century. | Laundresses--United States--Biography. | United States--History--Civil War, 1861-1865--Participation, Female. | Frontier and pioneer life--West (U.S.) | Laundry--United States--History--19th century. | United States. Army--Uniforms--History--Miscellanea.
Classification: LCC UB418.W65 L348 2016 | DDC 355.3/41--dc23
LC record available at http://lccn.loc.gov/2016003856

FIRST PRINTING
10 9 8 7 6 5 4 3 2 1
Manufactured in the United States of America

HIGH PLAINS PRESS
403 CASSA ROAD, GLENDO, WY 82213
WWW.HIGHPLAINSPRESS.COM
ORDERS & CATALOGS: 1-800-552-7819

To my husband Mark.
He has followed me to more forts and historical sites
than he ever imagined visiting
and has been supportive of my many endeavors.
Little did he know. . . .

Contents

Prologue: On Laundress Lane 11

1. Ladies and Lyes: Historical Perspectives 15

2. Laundry List: The Job 29

3. Ironing Out the Wrinkles: Benefits 47

4. Suds Row: Housing 63

5. The Baby and the Bathwater:
Family Life and Responsibilities 73

6. On the Side: Social Life 85

7. Extra Baggage:
Moving with the Troops 93

8. Dirty Laundry: The Darker Side 107

9. Out with the Wash Water:
The Decline and End 121

Appendix: Registry of Laundresses 127

Bibliography 139

Index 149

Acknowledgments 157

ON LAUNDRESS LANE

THE TOURISTS WALKED down the path leading to the laundress tents at the fort. I glanced around the area, making sure all the artifacts were in place. It was going to be a hot, humid day. A slight breeze was already blowing across the prairie. Smoothing my apron, I mentally slipped into character, becoming Kathleen Murphy, who, with my husband Sean, left Ireland in the midst of the potato famine to build a better life in the United States.

"Mornin'." I greeted them, with my best Irish brogue.

"Good morning." The woman gave me a skeptical glance. Then she got right to the point. "I understand that laundresses were actually prostitutes, hired to provide 'services' to the frontier soldiers." Her fingers curled into air quotes around the word "services" as she voiced the common assumption. It brought a smile to my face.

"No, ma'am. We are hired to do the laundry. That is not to say that some of my fellow laundresses didn't supplement their incomes by working as prostitutes, but that is definitely not part of the job. In fact, we can be fired and drummed off the post for that type of behavior."

I went on to explain the role of the laundress and her typical life. She was provided a minimum of supplies by the military, depending on the time period. She and her family were provided a place to live, however it was often some of the worst housing on the post. She received other benefits including a food ration, but was subject to military regulations and could be punished accordingly.

Laundresses typically made more money than their enlisted husbands. In fact, Elizabeth Custer referred to them as "a good investment" for their soldier husbands.

A laundress worked hard for her money. Much of her work was done outdoors. She had to be physically strong to carry the buckets of water, chop wood, and hand-wash heavy woolen uniforms. In addition, she probably had children to care for and all the duties of a homemaker of the time.

As I continued to visit with tourists throughout the day, the knowledge I had about this little-known group of women replayed in my head as I answered their many questions. I'd already discovered what little information is available on these washerwomen. I'd found entire books written about military uniforms of a certain time period without a single mention of the women who washed those uniforms or the methods used.

While women have always followed the troops, laundresses were the only women paid and recognized by the government for a period of time. They were sanctioned to serve from 1802 to 1876, after which they were slowly phased out of service. Some still received rations until 1883, and a few were provided modest housing until 1893. They were officially with the soldiers during the War of 1812, the Civil War, and the Indian Wars on the western frontier. They were among some of the first white and black women in the American West.

Laundresses played a vital role during those years. Not only did they wash uniforms, but some also cooked and cleaned for officers and their families, acted as midwives, cared for the sick and lonely, and provided a feminine presence. Some high-ranking officials felt the washerwomen added greatly to garrison life and made their husbands the best soldiers. For the most part, the laundresses were a good influence. The soldiers liked to see and talk to the women, and it made the men more content. There were strong arguments both for and against keeping the laundresses when the military decided to end the position.

A park service volunteer demonstrates the art of doing laundry for students on a grade school field trip. (National Park Service, San Juan National Historic Park)

A few laundresses made names for themselves, but it was not through ordinary work performed routinely. A Mexican-American War laundress, known as "the Great Northern," could outshoot most men. A well-known laundress from the Indian Wars period, Mrs. Nash, kept a secret that was not discovered until her death. Others were heroic or colorful or suffered misfortune. Because many of the laundresses were illiterate, what little we know comes only infrequently from the women themselves and most often from the writings of officers and their wives. The laundresses that "got written up" in the records, diaries, or newspapers were those who stood out in some way. No one made note of the laundresses who worked hard day after day, like Maggie Flood, who faced special family challenges on the frontier.

As the last car pulled out of the parking lot, I took off my bonnet, wiped the dust from around my eyes and contemplated how I could honor these unrecognized women. I made up my mind to start on the journey that became this book.

1. LADIES AND LYES

M **AGGIE FLOOD WAS** not your typical army laundress, but then perhaps there was no such thing. For Maggie Flood, her job as an army laundress was both a blessing and a curse. True, her work provided her growing family with a more predictable income than her husband, Patrick, ever had. But, it was miserable, backbreaking work with long hours that gave her little time for her family or herself.

Maggie, born in 1858 in Missouri, was a young teenager when she married Patrick Flood, a trooper with the Third U. S. Cavalry. By the time she was sixteen years old, she had moved with her husband to the windswept plains of Fort D. A. Russell, near Cheyenne, Wyoming. Their first son, John, was born at the fort on November 6, 1875.

By the time her second son, William, was born in 1877, Patrick had been transferred to Fort Laramie and Maggie followed. Records show Maggie as a laundress there in May 1878 working for Company A of the Third Cavalry. Maggie probably had taken the job to subsidize Patrick's unpredictable wages. Patrick's thirty-year military career suffered ups and downs as he moved through the ranks from private to sergeant and then back down again several times. Both his respect from fellow soldiers and his pay fluctuated with his rank, making it hard for Maggie to predict what tomorrow would bring.

Maggie continued working as a laundress even after their third son, Charles, was born in 1879 at Fort Laramie. The weather at the fort proved inhospitable with extremes ranging from over one hundred degrees in the summer to far below zero in the winter. Just keeping a family healthy and clean proved a challenge for any mother there, but Maggie took on the additional job of washing the laundry of soldiers using the primitive facilities along the Laramie River.

As if life hadn't provided Maggie with enough challenges, two of the Flood children, John and Charles, were deaf and needed special schooling. Maggie eventually saw that they were enrolled in the Nebraska School for the Deaf.

Maggie and Patrick's marriage was troubled. Patrick spent time in the stockade at least once for mistreating Maggie. Despite everything, Maggie and Patrick were still married and living at Fort McKinney, Wyoming, (near present-day Buffalo) when the census was taken in 1880; however, Maggie was then listed as the head of her household, while Patrick was listed as head of household for his barracks.

Eventually they divorced, and some better fortune came Maggie's way. She did something that few other military laundresses did—Maggie married an officer. She and her new husband, Captain Hamilton, moved to Washington, D.C., and later to California. More children followed, and the family lived a comfortable life.

—◈—

About one hundred years before Maggie Flood washed clothes at Fort Laramie, Sarah Osborn (also spelled Osborne) became one of the first military laundresses in what was to become the United States, serving the Patriots of the Continental Army during the Revolutionary War. In 1780 at the age of twenty-four, she had married Aaron Osborn, a man who had already served in early conflicts of the Revolutionary War. When he reenlisted as a commissary guard with the Third New York Regiment, he asked her to go with him. Though "laundress" was not then an official army designation, she received some benefits, was allowed to travel with the troops, and she washed clothes.

For three years she accompanied her husband's regiment. She took "her stand just back of the American tents . . . and busied herself washing, mending, and cooking."

*In this photograph, Maggie Flood, a laundress for thirty years begin-
ning in 1866, could easily pass for a contemporary grandmother. Yet
she had faced the challenges of a frontier laundress. Later she married
an officer and lived an easier life than the one she had in the frontier
West.* (Robert Flood)

Years later when she was eighty-one years old, Sarah applied for
a pension for Revolutionary War veterans and their widows. In her
deposition she gives a vivid account of the Battle of Yorktown, the
surrender of British General Cornwallis, and details of the day-to-
day life of a laundress and cook. She often "cooked and carried in
beef, and bread, and coffee (in a gallon pot) to the soldiers in the
entrenchment."

She says on one occasion when she was "carrying in provisions,"
she met General Washington, who asked her if she "was not afraid
of the cannonballs."

Kady Brownell could be called a vivandière. *During the U.S. Civil War she worked in a variety of military jobs, most likely including laundress.* (WikiCommons)

She replied, "No, the bullets would not cheat the gallows," joking that since she might well be hanged for supporting the Patriots, she had no reason to fear bullets. She continued: "It would not do for the men to fight and starve too."

The army provided Sarah with military transportation when the troops moved, something that mere camp followers were not granted. This demonstrated her value to the company.

After the war, Mr. Osborn abandoned Sarah and their children, and she later married another veteran, John Benjamin, and lived to be over one hundred years old. She received a double pension, likely one for each of her two husbands, but some believe that she should have been recognized for her own meritorious service.

Wars are a fact of life. For centuries, soldiers have gone off to fight, and throughout history, women have accompanied the men. Historically, they served as nurses, cooks, prostitutes, and even impromptu soldiers. However, one group, the laundresses, are the forgotten troopers of those wars. These women followed Napoleon Bonaparte's men across Europe, English soldiers around the world, and the American army from its inception until 1876, when laundresses were eliminated. Even so, it took several more years to phase them out.

The American army adopted the concept of military laundresses accompanying troops from the British army who had probably borrowed the idea from the French. In France, a woman attached to a military regiment was called a *vivandière* and served as a sutler by selling soldiers food, drink, and sundries beyond their basic rations. Some of the women adopted a uniform, which likely at first consisted of the cast-off military jacket of a soldier and later came to include more form-fitting jackets and perhaps a skirt with military trim worn over trousers.

In the early part of U.S. Civil War, a few regiments were accompanied by *vivandières*, who were sometimes identified as flag bearers or laundresses, and sometimes called "Daughters of the Regiment" or even "Mothers of the Regiment."

Although women of all sorts followed the army, only the laundresses were sanctioned by the military. All others, including the officers' wives, were most often designated as "camp followers," a somewhat derogatory term. Camp followers had no status in the realm of army life. Eventually, the military also added the title "hospital matron" as an official employee designation. The term hospital matron was often used interchangeably with laundress, and sometimes women served double duty as both.

Though a few women traveled as laundresses with the Continental Army, their superiors hadn't yet established a protocol for dealing with them. Their status was somewhat undefined. In September 1780, Captain George Fleming wrote to his superior officer,

Colonel Lamb, stating that he had recently lost a soldier named Peter Young. Young allegedly died as a result of "taking a large drink of cold water." Captain Fleming asked permission for Young's wife to continue as the company laundress, providing she wanted to keep the job.

In the same correspondence, Captain Fleming reported that soldier David Cornwall wanted his wife to be designated a laundress for the company also. Cornwall had asked Captain Fleming to attest that his wife was indeed already working as a washerwoman for the company. Fleming did so, adding that her husband behaved well, seemingly a recommendation.

In November of the same year, Captain Fleming confessed that he was unsure how to secure rations and provisions for his laundresses. He soon learned he could include them in the count when the company drew provisions. He added the two laundresses to the provisions count and later upped the number to four.

In 1778, the Second Pennsylvania Regiment set official rates that laundresses could charge for their services. Up until this time, the laundresses charged by the piece or set a wage, often reflecting the wages of other labor at the post. Overcharging prevailed, especially with piecework. Women who did not abide by the new regulations could be relieved of their duties, or worse, literally drummed out of the regiment in a public shaming.

An Act of Congress, on March 16, 1802, awarded the laundresses legal recognition and set more consistent practices. The ratio of laundresses to men was set at four laundresses to every one hundred men. However, it was not unusual for the numbers to vary. In the Continental Army, some units had carried up to twenty laundresses. In 1861, the regulations allowed four women per company, but the size of a company varied in number. Eventually the ratio was authorized at one laundress for every nineteen and one-half men.

After 1802, women who signed on as laundresses became "enrolled members" of the United States army. However, they were not obligated to stay with the army if they became unhappy in their

A group of refugee slaves (contrabands) with Union Army soldiers in front of General Lafayette's headquarters. (James Gibson, photographer. Library of Congress)

roles. Unlike soldiers, laundresses could leave at any time, with no fear of desertion charges. But in other aspects, their lives mirrored those of their male comrades.

During the War of 1812, some garrison regulations required that soldiers "will not wear their Fatique Frock & Trowsers more than three Days without washing." If enforced, this would have kept the laundresses extremely busy.

Army regulations of 1857 stated that the laundresses allowed to follow the army had to carry certificates, signed by the colonel, the Chief of the Corps, or a department officer. The women had to be of good character, though how this was assessed is unknown.

The captain of each company appointed not only his first sergeant, but also his laundress. Not all women appreciated the appointment. Years later in the frontier army at Fort Scott, Utah,

Patience Rozsa was not happy when her husband, John, came home and told her she was now on the company roll as a laundress. Patience complained that she had never done much laundry in her life. Consequently, John got up every morning at one or two o'clock and did the laundry, completing it by nine A.M. Several months later, another lady boarded with the Rozsas and agreed to do the laundry two days a week; she then worked for others the rest of the week. Eventually yet another woman took over and did the laundry for $2.50 a day.

A captain had the power to revoke a laundress's appointment for a variety of real or imagined wrongs. Although it was rare to have an appointment revoked, records show it did happen.

While a laundress was often married to an enlisted man, the mid-1800s government frowned upon married enlisted men in the army. In 1861, General Order No. 140 stated that while married men should not be excluded from the army, the number accepted should be determined by the number of laundresses needed in the companies.

Occasionally, a single woman signed on for the job. Records show there were twenty-three laundresses at Fort D. A. Russell, Cheyenne, Wyoming, in 1868. Sixteen of these women were married, two were daughters of laundresses, and five are assumed single by historians, as they did not bear the title "Mrs." in the records.

After the Civil War, most laundresses joined the army in the East and traveled with the troops to their station. These women became some of the first white women in some isolated areas of the West. As the country became more populated and the West more settled, women already residing in the frontier also became employed as laundresses.

The American army of the 1800s was a true reflection of the United States as a melting pot of nationalities. The birthplaces of many of the laundresses show this diversity. A close look at military records and this book's Laundress Registry (*Appendix*) shows military laundresses came from Ireland, England, Canada, Prussia (part of modern Germany), Bavaria (also part of Germany), Holland, Norwegia (Norway), France, Scandinavia, Italy and the United States. Elizabeth Anghey, a Canadian-born (1842) laundress, served at Fort Laramie, Wyoming, in 1870. Laundress Jane Baker was born in Prussia in 1825. Census rolls show she was a Fort Laramie laundress in 1860. Sarah Crisp was a U.S. citizen, born in New York. Ellen Coyle came from Ireland and served at Fort Laramie from 1880 to 1883.

Many laundresses came from Ireland. The Irish potato famine began in September 1845. By the time it ended in 1851, two million people had left Ireland. Many came to the United States only to discover it was not the land of opportunity. "Help Wanted" signs were common in Eastern cities, as was the caveat "Irish Need Not Apply." The army provided a small source of employment for the disenfranchised immigrants.

Native Americans found employment in various capacities at some forts, including as laundresses. Fort Totten, North Dakota, records indicate that Native American women did laundry, worked as servants and nannies, or in various other capacities at the fort for a dollar a day. As part of treaty agreements, Native American families often already received government rations, which were scheduled to arrive on a biweekly basis. However, the food and supplies did not last the families from one disbursement to the next. Hence, the women employed at the fort sometimes asked to be paid in kind, receiving additional meat, flour, sugar, and coffee to keep their families fed.

During the Civil War, soldiers' wives had first consideration for laundress positions, but, if positions went unfilled, other women, including both slaves and free blacks, worked as laundresses. Slaves turned their earnings over to their owners. Following Emancipation, black men signed on to become soldiers. The men often stayed with the army as the troops moved west, and the men in these segregated units earned the nickname "Buffalo Soldiers." Black women served as laundresses for the Buffalo Soldiers. Soldiers occasionally

Harper's Weekly *ran this drawing as part of an article on Our Women and War, on September 2, 1862. The title of the two-page spread is "The Influence of Woman." It shows nurses, laundresses, and a group of*

women making or mending shirts and socks. The laundress artwork is at the top right. Oftentimes the laundresses were called on to serve in all of these jobs because they were the only women available.

worked as laundresses, too. At the Civil War hospital in Cherokee Springs, Georgia, in 1863, a laundress and her soldier husband washed the laundry.

Prior to Emancipation, slaves sometimes served their owners in the military as cooks, laundresses, or nurses. Sometimes owners hired out their slaves to the military, but they did not change ownership or status. Southwestern forts also list Hispanic Americans as employees.

House Executive Documents show more laundresses were employed in the years 1873–1878 than during any other time period. The average number employed per year during this period was 1,740 women. This number corresponds with the westward expansion and the Indian Wars period in United States history. By 1880–1881, only 360 laundresses remained on army rolls.

Often neither laundresses nor their soldier husbands could read or write. Therefore, much of what is known about laundresses comes from a few personal accounts, military records, or the diaries of officers and their wives. Much of the record keeping was done at the company level, and few of those records remain. Information about laundresses is scarce in all cases. While they sometimes earned a mention for assisting an officer's wife in childbirth or other matters, the writings often reflect poorly on laundresses. Then, as now, the routine was not considered worth recording, but the unfortunate or unusual was remembered and documented.

The behavior of 1800s women mirrors the behavior of women today in basic ways. Some drank, fought with their husbands and with others, were dishonest, or engaged in prostitution or other unseemly ventures. For the most part, however, laundresses worked hard and led honest lives, caring for their families and participating in army life.

General George Forsyth claimed the laundresses were "good, honest, industrious" persons. An enlisted man, Private Ami F. Mulford, Company M, Seventh U. S. Cavalry, also appreciated the laundresses, describing them as "ladies in every sense of the word."

Other voices were not so kind. Various sources describe laundresses as a rough bunch of women, living in squalor, their quarters set amidst chickens, dogs, and other animals, all adding to the filth. Their children did not escape the wrath and were described as unkempt, uncared for, and dirty.

Despite hard work, primitive conditions, poor living quarters, and moving from fort to fort, employment as a laundress was not a terrible life for the times. A woman received military benefits, a home, and earned a fair wage. She had a paying job, something not easily found anywhere else.

1. LADIES AND LYES: *Bibliographical Notes*

Information in this chapter came from a variety of first-hand sources, military records, and published material. Robert Flood, great-grandson of Maggie Flood, provided information about Maggie's life and her photograph.

Throughout the book, when I found different spellings for a laundress's name, I used the earliest recorded spelling or that used most often.

Sarah Osborn(e)'s application for a Revolutionary War pension supplied much of the information about Osborn. It can be found at Record Group 15, Records of the Veterans Administration, National Archives, Washington, D.C.

The book *Glittering Misery: Dependents of the Indian Fighting Army* by Patricia Y. Stallard is a wonderful resource. Information about the early laundresses came from *Belonging to the Army: Camp Followers and Community During the American Revolution* by Holly Mayer and *The Art of Command: Military Leadership from George Washington to Colin Powell* by Harry Laver. Civil War information came from *The Encyclopedia of Civil War Medicine* by Glenna Schroeder-Lein, *Uniforms & Equipment of the Unites States Forces in the War of 1812* by Rene Chartand; and *Army Regulations Adopted for the Use of the Army of the Confederate States, in Accordance with Late Acts of Congress Revised from the Army Regulations of the old U.S. Army 1857.*

I also relied on an article in the December 10, 1985, issue of *History of the West,* "The Forgotten Women of the Frontier," by Sandra Hansen. Another article, with much information came from *Nebraska History,* 61(4), "Army Laundresses: Ladies of the 'Soap Suds Row,'" by Miller J. Stewart. *The Winterthur Portfolio 34,* Winter 1999, contains a useful article by A. K. Hoagland, "Village Constructions: U.S. Army Forts on the Plains, 1848-1890." I also found information in "Women of Johnston's Army" by Audrey M. Godfrey in the Spring 1986 issue of *Utah Historical Quarterly,* which added insight.

A useful website is "Fort Union and the Frontier Army in the Southwest: A Historic Resource Study, Fort Union National Monument Fort Union, New Mexico," by Leo E. Oliva.

More information about *vivandières* (sometimes called *cantinières*) can be found online and in the book *Intrepid Women: Cantinières and Vivandières of the French Army* by Thomas Cardoza.

The quotation from the Fort Wayne, Indiana, garrison regulation concerning washing uniforms every three days comes from the *Women Beyond the Frontier* by Willa G. Cramton.

Three other sources I recommend are *The Gentle Tamers* by Dee Brown; *The American Pageant, Seventh Edition;* and an Internet article, "The Roles Women Played in the War of 1812."

All of these references are listed in the complete bibliography at the end of this book.

I conducted personal research at several sites, primarily at Fort Laramie, Wyoming, and Fort Totten, North Dakota. I also read various volumes of Army Statutes at the University of Wyoming library.

2. LAUNDRY LIST

A LAUNDRESSES' JOB was wet, dirty, hard work. In early April 1864, while F Company, Seventh Iowa Cavalry was stationed near Cottonwood Springs, Nebraska, at Cantonment McKean (later renamed Fort McPherson), a sergeant suggested that a laundry would be a good idea so the men could wash their clothes, and his officers agreed. The men built a twenty-foot-square washhouse with cedar boxes for washtubs and other equipment. The water came from the nearby well at the horse corrals.

As fate would have it, shortly before the laundry was operational, a woman had dropped out of a westbound wagon train and sought employment at the nearby McDonald ranch. Mrs. McDonald eagerly employed her, as she had wanted to hire household help for some time. The woman, called by the nickname Lengthy, was no ordinary woman. Over six-feet tall, slim, and razor-faced, she gave the impression that she was afraid of nothing. Captain Nicholas J. O'Brien of F Company later described her: "She was ugly as a mud fence."

Lengthy had been raised on a Missouri farm. She was not married and probably had few prospects in Missouri, so she headed west. The homely woman originally planned to join some relatives living in Denver, Colorado. By the time she reached Cottonwood Springs, she decided she did not want to go any farther west. Lengthy was a hard worker and washed, cleaned, and did other work for the McDonalds. During this period, her nickname was shortened to "Linty."

Meanwhile, after the soldiers had washed their own clothes for a few months, the sergeant again approached his officers—this time about hiring a laundress, specifically Linty. All of Company F agreed to her appointment as the company laundress. She was added to the roll and moved into the washhouse. Linty curtained off quarters in the new building for her bed and trunk. She continued to be very hardworking and was an excellent laundress. The McDonalds were disappointed to lose her.

In May, the sergeant who had suggested hiring Linty asked for her hand in marriage. The captain, although unsure about his authority to do so, married the couple. In the tradition of the period, about a hundred soldiers charivaried the new couple, surrounding the washhouse on the wedding night, banging on pots and pans and hollering. The noise suddenly stopped when the sergeant went through Linty's pockets and found five dollars. He gave the money to the men, telling them to go get drunk.

The sergeant had acquired a wife who added both rations and pay to his household. He also started living in her quarters in the washhouse.

This did not sit well with the officers. They immediately reduced the sergeant in rank and sent him off the post on less-than-desirable duty, repairing wagons and shoeing horses. This did not affect their marriage, however. Linty and the sergeant stayed married. She accompanied the men on all of their marches and expeditions, no matter how dangerous. Because of her hard work and devotion to the unit, she became a highly respected member of Company F, Seventh Iowa Cavalry. The men in the unit were said to have more respect for her than they did for her husband.

⊰⊱

Emily FitzGerald, wife of an army doctor, was offered comfort and support by two laundresses in Sitka, Alaska, in 1874. By her own accounts, Emily was quite lonely when her husband John went out on campaign. She preferred to have him home, but his services were required in the field even during the time Emily was expecting their second child. So Emily depended upon the laundresses. A laundress named Mrs. Smith, the wife of a soldier, agreed to help

This life-sized bronze honoring laundresses shows a woman using a sad iron. It is part of the display at the Corinth Contraband Camp in Mississipi. Considered a "model" camp, it was run by the Union Army for newly-freed slaves who sought refuge with the Union troops. At one time the Corinth camp had up to 6,000 residents. Many of the blacks were absorbed into the army as laundresses, cooks, and teamsters. Others worked as laundresses within the camp. (National Park Service, National Military Park, Corinth, MS)

Emily when the baby was born and to stay with her at night for the first week after the birth. Mrs. Smith also agreed to help during her free time for a few weeks after that. Another laundress agreed to help Emily when Mrs. Smith was busy with her work. Both of these women also continued to do their regular laundry work.

The birth of the FitzGeralds' new baby Herbert ("Bertie") went smoothly, but less than two weeks later, Emily took ill with peritonitis. Mrs. Smith was called on again to help with the children while Emily recovered. The army had no designation for a "nanny," so the laundresses willingly helped out as they could. FitzGerald thought the world of both women, calling them "gems."

❦

Doing the laundry was a drawn out affair, taking the better part of the week. The laundress washed for the troops and her own family and sometimes washed for officers and their families.

Lack of adequate laundry facilities added to the burden, although the facilities varied over time and from location to location. During the Civil War, hospitals required a large number of laundresses. The surgeon in charge decided whether the laundresses worked on hospital grounds or if they took the hospital laundry back to their tents. If the laundress worked on the grounds, shelter might consist of buildings, tents, sheds, or trees. A Confederate surgeon in Kingston, Georgia, did not provide his laundresses with any facilities at all. Because his grandmother and mother always washed outside with no shelter, he expected his laundresses to do the same and gave them no protection from the weather.

Similar conditions existed on the western frontier. At some posts the army provided laundresses with only a second wall tent to use as a washing facility. Wooden or adobe buildings served as washhouses in some places. The hovels that housed many laundresses at the various forts left little room for doing laundry in their "homes." Trees were in short supply across much of the west and were not a reliable source of shade or shelter on military posts.

In most cases, laundresses provided their own supplies. The Continental Army supplied laundresses with fat from the slaughterhouses and a wooden cask to use in making their soap. On the frontier most sutlers' stores sold soap, but it was expensive. So laundresses made their own, using animal fat and lye. The women saved kitchen fat. In addition, if the fort had a slaughterhouse, butchered animals provided a ready source of fat.

⸺◈⸺

Making Lye. Lye is an alkaline liquid made from rainwater and ashes. An experienced laundress knew that all ash was not the same. The ash from oak and other hardwood produced the strongest solution. Some ash resulted in lye that discolored light colored clothing, but was fine for dark clothing. Applewood was thought to produce the whitest wash.

To make lye, women mixed ash and water in a wooden keg. Periodically, they drew off the liquid, added more ash, and poured the liquid back over the ash. The more often this occurred, the stronger the resulting lye. After following the process over a few days, the laundress tested the lye for strength. If a raw potato or egg floated in the liquid, it was sufficiently strong to make soap. Next the laundress filtered the mixture to remove the ash and stored the resulting lye in either glass or wooden containers. Obviously she saved time and effort if she could purchase powdered lye. On the frontier the sutler's store sometimes carried it, but at discouraging prices.

Straight lye made an excellent spot treatment prior to washing and sometimes was used as a washing solution in place of soap, particularly for white items and children's clothing.

If used as a substitute for soap, the lye was diluted, often with sour milk, before washing clothes. The woman put clothes or linens loosely in the washtub with sticks placed among the items to keep them from packing together. She slowly poured the lye solution over the clothing and drew it off from the bottom. She repeated this with a new solution until the lye came out clean. Then she rinsed the clothes or linens and put them out to dry. She did have to be careful, as full strength lye, improperly used, could potentially destroy the garments.

Rendering Fat. The next step in soap making was rendering the meat fat. The laundress removed as much meat and other matter from the raw fat as possible. She cut it into small pieces and cooked it until it liquefied. She then strained out all remaining solids and saved the meat solids for use in later cooking.

Making Soap. Next, the laundress poured the clarified fat back into the iron kettle and slowly added water. She heated the mixture over the fire, stirring it with a wooden paddle or another wooden utensil until it was well blended. Then she carefully added the lye, slowly stirring it. She brought the mixture to a low boil and cooked it for thirty minutes to an hour, stirring occasionally.

Experience helped the laundress determine when the soap was ready. As it cooked it became thick and creamy. It was finished once it ran off the paddle in sheets without any clear liquid visible.

Then she poured the soap into a mold, which was often a simple wooden box. After the soap hardened she cut it into bars. [Many people think lye soap is very harsh, but this is not true. It has close to a neutral pH, as the harsh alkaline lye breaks down in the cooking process.]

Sorting. Usually, the laundress gathered and sorted clothes the day before she planned to wash. She sorted the clothes into groups according to the order they would be washed: light whites, heavy whites, colored cottons, light wools, and heavy wools.

Getting water. With the lye and soap made and the clothes sorted, a laundress began her washday by getting water, often hauled from a creek or river. This water was not always sanitary. At Fort Laramie, Wyoming, a commander dealt with the manure and slaughterhouse

By the 1880s, laundry soap powder was available at every grocery store according to this advertisement, but army laundresses on isolated posts often did not have access to either grocery stores or commercial soap powder. (Library of Congress)

offal by ordering it dumped into the Laramie River. Considerately, he requested it be dumped downriver from the area where soldiers bathed and laundresses fetched their water.

Getting water from a creek was dangerous. In the winter, the creek often froze over, making it necessary to chop ice. A slip of the axe could result in injury, which sometimes had serious consequences. Wounds often became infected, which could lead to the laundress being unable to work and draw wages. Occasionally a wound became gangrenous, which might lead to amputation or even death.

In the spring, the creek water ran high and fast. If a laundress was pulled into the current, in all likelihood she would drown, dragged under by her heavy and bulky clothing. Fort Laramie, for

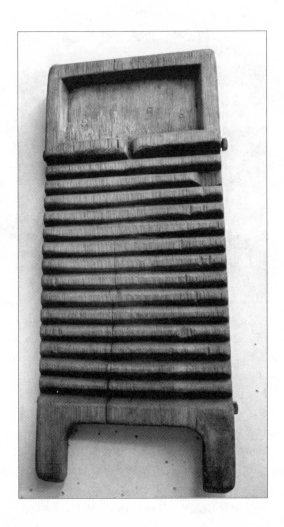

Washboards were used to rub the dirt from clothing. Traditionally they were made from wood, but several types of metal were also used. Different designs were unique enough that some were patented; others were handmade.

example, sat at the confluence of the Laramie and North Platte Rivers. Both adults and children drowned on occasion in these rivers.

Conversely, in the late summer and fall the water levels fell and water became harder to secure.

Some forts had wells, often located near the kitchens, for the inhabitants' use. A well eliminated the hazards of hauling water from a creek or river, but it still required heavy, laborious work. Each cauldron held eighteen to twenty gallons of water or more. A laundress hauled at least sixty to one hundred gallons of water for all the wash, which weighed approximately five hundred to eight hundred pounds collectively. The women hauled the water in buckets, sometimes using a yoke to make them somewhat easier to carry.

Wood. Laundresses heated the water over a wood fire. The wood used as fuel varied depending on what was available in the geographic area. At western forts where wood was scarce, parties of soldiers, called wood details, went out to find and cut wood for heating and washing.

The wood burned at Fort Laramie came from cottonwood, juniper, ponderosa pine, ash, and box elder. The amount of wood needed at the fort was phenomenal. In 1866, Major James Van Voast predicted that it would take 1,550 cords of wood just to keep the fort going for the winter. A cord of wood measures four foot high by four foot wide by eight foot long. Other forts required similarly massive amounts of wood. Because of this heavy demand, soon all the nearby available trees had been cut, and wood details had to travel ten to fifteen miles or more from the fort to find wood. Soldiers working away from the fort made easy targets for those opposed to their presence.

After the wood arrived at the forts, soldiers off-loaded it from the wagons into piles for each company. Soldiers cut it into appropriate lengths for use in their barracks, in the officers' quarters, and kitchens. However, laundresses had to chop their own firewood. Many of the same hazards that applied to chopping ice applied to

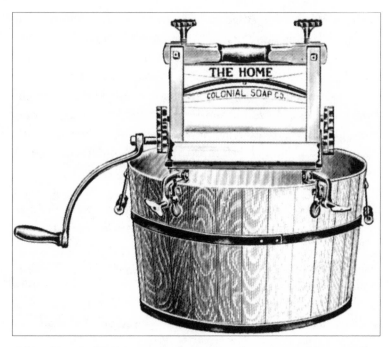

A hand-cranked wringer was a luxury laundresses coveted but not all had the opportunity to own. This is an 1800s catalog image.

chopping firewood. In addition, in dry climates the axe handles shrank, and the axe heads came loose and could fly off. Soaking the handle in water helped prevent this shrinkage.

Soldiers and laundresses split wood on a chopping block. Rather than attempting to split the length of the wood down the middle, they shaved off each of the four sides first. This provided kindling and smaller pieces of wood. If necessary, they cut down the block of wood again, using the same methods. Squared off logs also stacked more easily and efficiently.

Tools. The equipment that laundresses used was not all standard issue. What was supplied to them by the military varied over time, and the women often made do with what was available or adapted tools from other uses.

Laundresses often heated the water in eighteen to twenty gallon (or larger) iron or copper cauldrons, commonly referred to as coppers. These could also serve as washtubs.

Other tools made a laundress's job easier, as well. Some washer-women used a "washing dolly," a long wooden pole with four wooden pegs at the bottom, to agitate clothes. Two horizontal handles at the top helped the laundress stir and move the clothes through the wash water.

Early laundresses used laundry bats to clean the clothing. They pounded the clothing with the bat to clean it.

The first United States patent for a washboard was applied for in 1833. After that, laundresses used washboards made with the traditional wood, or copper, sheet iron, tin, or zinc, to rub dirt from the clothing. She submerged the ribbed part into her tubs, leaned into the top to hold it steady, and scrubbed the clothing against the ribs. Washboards were sometimes mockingly referred to as "army pianos," probably because they were sometimes used as makeshift musical instruments.

Washing. The general order of washing consisted of presoaking, washing with soap, a first rinse in warm or boiling water, a second rinse of cool water, and perhaps a third rinse. White clothes took more steps: they were presoaked, rubbed on the washboard, and spot-treated as needed, assuming they were not cleaned strictly with a lye solution. Then the laundress stoked up the fire and boiled the whites in soapy water for approximately an hour. Using a knife, the laundresses flaked soap off the bar to create quicker, more evenly distributed, suds.

Following the soapy wash, the laundress used her dolly stick or large wooden tongs to move the clothes into the first rinse. The boiling water further agitated the clothes and forced soap through the fibers. However, care was taken with the boiling rinse because colored clothes faded in hot water and, since all clothing was made of natural fibers like cotton or wool, clothes would shrink if left in hot water for too long. For this reason, many clothes were rinsed in warm water. Sometimes laundresses soaked colored items in salt to keep the colors from fading and running. The second rinse was cool water. The final rinse was cool water and often included a bluing agent to make the whites brighter.

If the laundress had a hand-cranked wringer, or mangle, she clamped it onto the washtub, making wringing out the clothes a bit easier. If she did not, she wrung the wet clothes by hand, sometimes twisting them around a pole to help remove excess water.

Washing woolen garments constituted the bulk of a military laundress's work. The soldiers' standard issue uniforms were made of wool, as were many other garments of the time. The garments shrank in hot water. Over-scrubbing or wringing the soapy clothes too tightly caused the fibers to felt. Occasionally a laundress inadvertently damaged or ruined clothing by careless washing, and if that happened the laundress was responsible for the damage done. Woolen garments were not presoaked because of the possibility of damage. These clothes went directly into the wash kettle, containing warm water, soap, and ammonia. (Human urine and processed hog manure were frequent sources of ammonia.) The laundress used an agitator to move the garments through the wash water and to gently lift them up and down. Then she carefully squeezed the soapy water from the clothing and rinsed them two or three more times in cool water. Then she gently wrung out the excess water, shook the clothes, and hung them or laid them out to dry.

A second method of cleaning woolen garments consisted of surface cleaning. The laundress sponged a mixture of ammonia and water onto the garment, rinsed it in warm water, and gingerly wrung out the excess moisture. Sometimes laundresses shared recipes for cleaning solutions between friends. Some contained dangerous chemicals, and the effectiveness of others is doubtful.

Drying. The laundress hung the wash to dry if she had a clothesline. However, as all people who have used a clothesline know, weather

Many times army laundresses wrung wet clothes by hand or with a hand-cranked wringer that attached to the side of a tub. However, army hospital laundresses by the 1880s may have used more heavy-duty machines. (Blandford Town Museum)

plays havoc with laundry hung outside. The wind whipped garments on the line, blew clothing away, and could tear and physically destroy things. Dust storms quickly undid all the laundresses' hard work. In the winter, the clothing froze on the line before drying.

Another method of drying laundry involved laying it over bushes or shrubs or spreading it out on a clean, grassy area if one were

A sampling of irons. 1. Box irons opened to a hollow body. A heated slug was placed within the body. If the iron had vents on the side, fuel could be placed inside. 2. An accomplished ironer needed a variety of irons. 3. Sad irons were cast with the handle attached and some were pointed on both ends. 4. This small iron was for collars, cuffs, and lace. It was sometimes called a "child's iron." 5. Mary Potts patented an iron with a detachable wooden handle.

available. But suitable areas were scarce given the primitive nature of a laundress's work and living areas.

Drying the clothes outside was preferable to indoor drying in many ways. The sun helped bleach white clothing, and the fresh air helped eliminate odors. If necessary, laundresses hung clothing inside, but this created a crowded, damp environment, making the job even more difficult.

Repairing. Once the clothes were dry, the laundress reattached any loose or missing buttons and mended small tears. She had repaired the most noticeable damage before laundering to prevent further harm to the clothing. Laundresses were sometimes allowed to charge more per item when repairs were made.

Ironing. Ironing came next. Irons ranged in weight from a few ounces to nine or more pounds, with different sizes used for different tasks. The smallest irons were designed for collars, cuffs, and lace. Young girls often helped their mothers with the ironing. These small-sized irons proved perfect for small hands, both for work and play, and were given the name "child's iron." The largest irons were used on coats and other heavy items. Special irons made pressing pleated or gathered fabric easier.

During the first part of the nineteenth century, two types of irons were commonly used. The box iron had a hollow body, with a hinged or sliding heel plate or top. A cast iron slug was heated in the fire and placed within the body. Each iron came with two slugs, so one could be heating while the other was being used. Since the slug did not come in contact with the clothes, these irons did not tend to dirty the clothing.

A similar type of box iron had a deep, hollow body that held charcoal or other burning fuel. Vents located on the side of the body helped keep charcoal or embers burning. The laundress either blew on them to increase the heat, or she swung the iron back and forth to force air through the vents.

The second, and more popular iron in the 1800s, was the sad iron, also called a flat iron. Cast as a solid piece, the handle was permanently attached to the iron. A laundress needed two flat irons, so she could use one while the other heated. To heat them, she propped them up, bottom plate towards the fire or suspended them from a hook above the fire. Their cast iron handles became very hot so laundresses padded both the handles and their hands to prevent burns.

In 1871, Mary Potts, of the United States, patented a new type of iron. The cast iron base, or body, was pointed at both ends with a detachable, wooden handle. A set of these new irons came with three bases, a handle, and a trivet for resting the hot iron. These irons were heated and used much the same as others.

Because none of these irons had temperature settings, they could get extremely hot. A good laundress knew when the temperature was right. However, she commonly tested the iron on a scrap of cloth before using it on clothing.

The laundress laid a plank of wood between two stumps, chairs, or whatever could be improvised to create an ironing board. She added padding made with old blankets or sheets.

⊰◈⊱

Once the laundry was finished, the laundress cleaned and cared for her equipment. Her responsibilities did not end there.

Laundresses were often pressed into service to nurse the sick and wounded. This was particularly true during the Civil War. Laundresses from both the North and the South assumed nursing duties in the field and in hospitals. After a battle, when a large number of wounded suddenly needed care, laundresses were pressed into duty as nurses. Few laundresses received recognition for nursing, but they did what needed to be done.

A laundress with a husband and family maintained her own living quarters and cooked for her own family.

But as difficult as the job of washing clothes was, a laundress was comparatively well compensated and received rations and housing. For the time, it was considered a decent job.

2. LAUNDRY LIST: *Bibliographical Notes*

An Army Doctor's Wife on the Frontier: The Letters of Emily Mc-Corkle FitzGerald from Alaska and the Far West 1874-1878 by Emily FitzGerald provided important information for this chapter. *Laundry Bygones,* by Pamela Sambrook, was a major source of information, as was *Crinolines and Crimping Irons: Victorian Clothes How They Were Cleaned and Cared For* by Christina Walkley and Vanda Foster.

I am grateful for information from *Glittering Misery: Dependents of the Indian Fighting Army* by Patricia Y. Stallard, *The Gentle Tamers* by Dee Brown; *Chimborazo: The Confederacy's Largest Hospital* by Carol Green; and *The Encyclopedia of Civil War Medicine* by Glenna R. Schroeder-Lein.

Additional information on "Linty" came from *The Indian War of 1864* by Eugene Ware. Information on sources of ammonia came from "Victorian Laundry (or Aren't You Glad You Didn't Live Then?)" with full source data in the bibliography.

I also used information from "Fort Laramie: Part 5 Life of the Soldier" by David Lavender, in *U.S. History* magazine and "Army Laundresses: Ladies of the 'Soap Suds Row'" by Miller J. Stewart, in *Nebraska History.*

I conducted personal on-site research at Fort Buford, North Dakota, and Fort Laramie, Wyoming.

3. Iron Out the Wrinkles

A T THE AGE OF fourteen, Susie King Taylor lived with the constant smell of gunpowder, campfire smoke, and blood. In October of that year, 1862, young Susie had become the regimental laundress for all black First South Carolina Volunteers (Thirty-third United States Colored Troops.)

Taylor was an anomaly. Born under slave law in Georgia in 1848 as Susan Baker, she was one of the few slaves to have the opportunity to learn to read and write. This proved to be a great asset to her, not only as a laundress during the Civil War, but for the rest of her life as well.

Taylor was born on the Grest Farm, approximately thirty-five miles from Savannah, Georgia. Mrs. Grest was quite fond of Susie and her brother and often had them sleep at the foot of her bed. When Susie was seven years old, Mr. Grest allowed the children's grandmother to take Susie and her brother to live in Savannah. Her grandmother saw to it that Susie attended a school secretly run by a free woman, even though formal education for blacks was against the law at that time. Susie wrapped her books in plain paper to keep the police and white people from seeing them as she walked to school. Her education continued sporadically with other teachers, including a white playmate who attended a convent school and taught Susie what she learned there.

In April 1862, Taylor was sent back to live with her mother. Soon, she fled with her uncle and his family and other blacks to

Saint Catherine Island and then to Saint Simon Island where they received the protection of Union officials. When officers learned of her ability to read and write, she was asked to organize and take charge of a children's school on the island. So at age 14, she became the first African-American to openly teach freed black children in Georgia. While at Saint Simon, she married Edward King, a sergeant in Company E.

In later life, Susie wrote a memoir, *Reminiscences of My Life in Camp*, which focuses on her military life.

Saint Simon was soon evacuated and the regiment transferred to Beaufort, South Carolina, in October. At that time Susie was enrolled as a laundress for the Union Army. When smallpox broke out, she nursed at least one ill soldier in the evenings. Despite her care, along with the doctor and camp steward's care, the man died. She also taught off-duty soldiers to read and write. She served as a laundress, nurse, cook, and teacher for over four years "without receiving a dollar" of compensation, she writes. She says she was just happy to be allowed to accompany the troops.

Camp life was brutal. It was cold in the winter. Taylor writes of nearly being eaten alive by fleas in the summer, causing her to vacate her tent and stay up all night, and she tells of a fear of stepping on snakes. In addition, she describes the horrors of the war.

In July 1863, Union troops made their famous charge of Fort Wagner on Morris Island, which protected the port of Charleston. In anticipation of this, she helped as many soldiers as possible pack their haversacks with hard tack, salt beef, and canteens of water. Each man was also allowed a cartridge box with 150 rounds. Following the charge, Taylor devoted her time to caring for the wounded as they arrived. Men were missing arms and legs, and many had serious wounds to their feet. Over half of the all black regiment was killed. In her book, she says she did very little laundry because she was always doing something of higher priority for the officers and comrades.

She continued to travel and serve the troops for three more years. Despite the war, there were occasional moments of levity in

Susie King Taylor is perhaps the most distinguished of the army laundresses. She attended school and later taught soldiers to read. She was the only known black woman to write and publish her memories of Civil War army life. (Library of Congress)

camp. The drummer boys took care of a pig, which became the pet of the camp. The pig would march out with them, and they taught him tricks. They took special delight in disrupting the evening prayer meeting by riding the pig through the services.

On February 9, 1866, the regiment was finally mustered out. Taylor and her husband returned to Savannah. He died later that year, leaving her with a small child. She held a variety of jobs during the remainder of her life, including laundress, cook, and teacher.

Few women recorded military life during this period, and even fewer of those women came from the enlisted ranks. Taylor is the only known black woman to write and publish her memories of Civil War army life.

⟨⟩

While Susie King Taylor was well educated, in that era most black people were not. Both Confederate and Union officers spoke freely in front of African American servants and left documents and maps where the servants could see them, assuming the slaves and servants would not understand what they were seeing and hearing. This was not always the case.

One of the most famous Civil War spies was the well-known black woman Harriet Tubman who is often chronicled as a cook, nurse, laundress, and humanitarian.

However, a lesser-known married couple also proved themselves clever Union spies while doing laundry. In 1863, a runaway slave named Dabney and his wife joined Union forces led by General Joseph Hooker. Dabney worked in Hooker's camp as a cook and servant. His wife left the camp after a short stay and returned to the Confederate side of the river. She quickly found employment as a laundress and personal servant for a woman where her duties included washing clothes for Confederate officers in Fredericksburg.

Shortly thereafter, Dabney began supplying Hooker with information about the Confederate troop movements. His reports were a wealth of information. He seemed to know what units were moving, where they had been and where they were going, the size of the units, and more. The information was extremely accurate.

No one could figure out how Dabney was getting this information. Despite the fact that he had a good knowledge of the surrounding countryside, he was always busy with his duties and was never seen leaving the camp. Finally, after much questioning, he told the officers his secret. He led them to a vantage point overlooking Fredericksburg and the Confederate side of the river. He pointed across the river to a small house on the outskirts of the city. He explained that the clothesline in the yard of the house was a type of telegraph. His wife, who washed and cooked for Confederate officers there, had a system for hanging the laundry that told Dabney what the troops were doing.

"Well," Dabney said to the Union officers, "that clothesline tells me in half an hour just what goes on at Lee's headquarters. You see my wife over there? She washes for the officers, cooks, and waits around, and as soon as she hears about any movement or anything going on she comes down and moves the clothes on that line so I can understand it in a minute. That there gray shirt is Longstreet; and when she takes it off [the line], it means he's gone down about Richmond. That white shirt means Hill; and when she moves it up to the west end of the line, Hill's corps has moved up stream. That red one is Stonewall Jackson. He's down on the right now, and if he moves, she'll move that red shirt."

The Dabneys had worked out a complicated system using the laundry as a code. In addition to the aforementioned signals, there were others. For example, an upside down pair of pants signaled westward movement and two blankets pinned together at the bottom represented a trap. Because of the Dabneys, Confederate dirty laundry proved to be more than just laundry.

⊰◈⊱

The benefits provided an attractive reward for the hard labor involved in being a laundress. Although pay scales and benefits varied over time and from post to post, the women often earned more than the average enlisted man. As a company laundress, a woman made a

This period cartoon characterization captures one common perception of an army laundress—a rugged, smoking, drinking, independent woman. In reality, laundresses could not be stereotyped. (Vanity Fair, November 2, 1861)

contribution to the family both through income and food. Elizabeth Bacon Custer summed it up by saying marrying a laundress was a good investment for an enlisted man. Income earned for washing, along with the extra rations allotted by the military, plus other benefits, allowed the family of a soldier with a laundress for a wife to live in relative comfort.

During the American Revolution, though women were present in the military camps doing cooking, nursing, and laundry, they were not recognized as actual members of the military. George Washington did not like having the women around; however, he realized that if he ordered them to leave, their husbands might also leave. At that time, although "laundress" was not a well-defined position, some drew rations, and the Army established a pay scale for their services. A woman mostly did work for her own family and for soldiers in her husband's unit. If a soldier-husband was killed, the woman was usually required to leave.

When Congress recognized military laundresses in 1802, the women began to receive somewhat standard pay and benefits. A company was provided a ration for each person on its rolls. This act required that each bona fide laundress receive one ration. At that time, the daily ration was valued at twenty cents, later raised by 1857 to thirty cents a day. The number of men in a company varied, but typically ranged between sixty-five and one hundred, and after 1802 laundresses were included in the ration counts.

The items in the food ration varied, based on what was available at the time. The standard ration included meat, bread, and whiskey, but those could fluctuate depending on what could be purchased locally. For instance, when pork was available, a ration of twelve-ounces of pork per day for each person was distributed. Salt pork and sowbelly were the most common forms of pork.

In 1870, the food ration per person was "meat (twelve ounces of salt pork or bacon,) or twenty ounces of beef (fresh, salted, or canned); eighteen ounces of flour or fresh bread, or twelve ounces of hardbread, or sixteen ounces of cornmeal; 2.4 ounces of beans or peas, or 1.6 ounces of hominy or rice; 1.6 ounces of coffee or 0.32 ounces of tea; 2.4 ounces of sugar, and small amounts of salt, pepper, and vinegar." The ration also included soap and candles.

Often rations were figured per one hundred people. Beans were issued in fifteen-pound lots and rice in ten-pound lots. The flour ration varied. Before the Civil War, each person received eighteen ounces of flour per day. During the war, it increased to twenty-two ounces, then was cut back again to eighteen ounces for economic reasons. The post Administrative Council had the right to adjust this amount at their discretion. For instance, if potatoes and onions were not available, the council had the option of increasing the flour ration. This happened on occasion at Fort Laramie, particularly toward the end of winter when vegetables were in short supply. When vegetables became available again, flour was cut back.

Laundresses obtained a few days' rations at one time. The menu, however, tended to be quite monotonous. Mrs. Fred Klawitter, wife of an enlisted man at Fort Abraham Lincoln, North Dakota, in the 1870s, made do with the standard rations. At that time, the menu consisted of bacon, beans, hardtack, and beef. She longed for fresh eggs to no avail.

Private Wilmont Sanford, of Fort Buford, North Dakota, kept track of his diet in a journal. On Sunday, September 2, (probably 1877), he had potatoes and beef for the noon meal. On Wednesday, September 20, he had potatoes and beans. Tuesday, October 6 was similar. For breakfast he had steak and potatoes and for lunch, soup. On Wednesday, October 14, breakfast consisted of bacon, and the noon meal consisted of mashed potatoes and steak. Thursday, October 22, showed a bit of variety; he listed pork for breakfast, potatoes and cabbage for dinner, and apples for supper.

Boiling was a popular method of cooking. Salted meats were usually boiled to remove some salt. Beans and rice were also boiled. Bacon, or sowbelly, was often rancid or rotten by the time the soldiers and laundresses received it, and boiling helped sterilize it. Stew or hash, made with the salted meats and slow cooked overnight in a heavy, iron kettle, was one way of providing a bit of variety in the menu. When fresh meat was available, it was generally roasted or fried.

While sailors had already discovered citrus fruits as a way to control scurvy, the harsh conditions of western forts, short growing seasons, and long hauls on freight wagons prevented the inclusion

Not all army laundresses traveled with troops and lived at isolated posts. The Union Army ran 20-25 hospitals in Nashville during the Civil War and even more in Philadelphia. That created a lot of laundry and a need for laundresses. The laundresses in the photograph are believed to be at "Pest House" which treated prostitutes and was run by the military. (National Archives, Washington D.C.)

of many scurvy-preventing foods into the diet. Packing and storage, along with poor preservation techniques, led to a multitude of problems, including moldy or rotten food. In 1868, the post surgeon at Fort Buford noted there were thirty-four cases of scurvy during the winter and spring.

On the western frontier, the surgeon general ordered that gardens be planted at the posts; this met with varying success. At Fort Laramie, the soil was poor, hail was a given in the summer, frosts arrived as early as August, and grasshoppers sometimes ate the plants to nubs—gardening was a challenge. One officer doubted whether enough food could be raised in the gardens to make the effort worthwhile. At Fort Lincoln, North Dakota, better growing conditions allowed for more success with gardening. At Fort Harker, Kansas, in 1869, the post garden hosted twenty-two different vegetables and herbs, including parsley and thyme. Soldiers planted most of the common garden vegetables including watermelon.

Assistant Post Surgeon Kimball, at Fort Buford, chronicled the growth of that post's garden in 1868. The garden covered five acres of ground. On July 3, it was producing enough lettuce and radishes to feed everyone at the post. Lamb's Quarter, an indigenous edible plant, was also in good supply. On July 22, Kimball noted that grasshoppers had appeared in large numbers. Potato bugs also presented problems. An unnamed insect was attacking the cabbage. By this time, the peas were ready to harvest, along with the cucumbers and onions. Again, the plants were prolific, and the occupants of the post were well fed from the garden. The surgeon noted that cucumbers seemed to grow better than anything else. A storm on July 25 took care of the grasshopper problem, but not before serious damage had been done to the beans, peas, and spinach. In August, the people again ate well from the garden, however the potato crop was a complete failure. Assistant Post Surgeon Kimball continued his garden records the following year. At the end of May he noted that it had rained occasionally, and the garden looked quite promising.

Soldiers' wives, presumably mainly laundresses, canned the bulk of the garden produce and made jams and jellies for consumption in the winter. Sometimes officers' wives and their servants joined in the preserving.

As early as the Civil War, desiccated vegetables in cakes or plugs supplemented diets. On the western frontier, government freighters brought in these dried vegetables to all the forts. Drying the vegetables and pressing them kept them from spoiling and made them lightweight and easy to freight. The mixture consisted of a variety of vegetables, including onions, cabbage, peas, celery, carrots, beets, turnips, tomatoes, and peppers. A standard vegetable cake was approximately nine inches by three inches and approximately an inch thick. These vegetable bricks were simmered in water until they softened and expanded. They became more palatable if they were added to soup or stew and simmered even longer. Then, as now, potatoes came dried and powdered. The potato powder was mixed with water, formed into cakes, and fried.

A laundress could sometimes buy additional flour or other supplies for her family. However, at Fort Phil Kearny, Wyoming, during one year, flour fell into short supply before summer. Orders were issued controlling the sale of flour to laundresses. Flour for children's meals was also rationed. The health and nutrition of the soldiers was the uppermost priority.

Many factors governed food availability at both the post commissary and the sutler's store. Weather was a major factor, especially in the winter, but also when thaws or rains made trails impassable for freight wagons. In 1867, residents of Fort C. F. Smith, Montana, experienced food shortages because of severe weather. In addition, Indians constantly attacked the fort and the trail to the fort. Both factors prevented food from being delivered.

Often contractors created the problem. Seeing the army as a ready source of money, unscrupulous contractors supplied the cheapest food they could obtain and thought nothing of sending outdated stock. George Armstrong Custer described a shipment of bread, baked in 1861, shipped to his soldiers in 1867. The same shipment included well-sealed boxes shipped from a supply depot. The boxes contained rocks. The government paid by the pound to ship these boxes.

Even when food was available it was often unsanitary. Pests infested the supplies. Insects thrived in the flour and cornmeal. Cooks routinely found rat and mouse droppings in bags of flour and grain. Now and then, a mouse body had to be picked out before cooking. Cooks sifted out maggots, weevils, and worms routinely.

Occasionally laundresses received an issue of equipment. Continental Army laundresses were given fat from the slaughterhouse and a wooden cask for making soap. In 1841, army regulations deemed that each group of four laundresses would be provided the following equipment: one common tent, one hatchet, one camp kettle, and two mess pans. Presumably, the first three items were shared laundry equipment.

Once the position was authorized, infrequently a laundress received financial compensation directly from the army, but the system and the amount varied from year to year and could vary with the economy. During the Civil War, the head surgeon hired many laundresses to wash bedding and other laundry at the war hospitals. One laundress washed for twenty men. Union laundresses received six dollars a month, while Confederate laundresses were paid eight dollars a month. Both sides provided a daily ration for these laundresses. War hospitals had poor working conditions, generated filthy laundry, were oftentimes dangerous, and the pay was relatively low. The military found it hard to hire and keep good laundresses during the Civil War.

A guaranteed wage provided the big incentive for laundresses after the Civil War. The post Administrative Council (often the three senior officers at the garrison) established the rates at each fort and, in all cases, the pay was considered good. The pay scale reflected the average wage for unskilled civilian labor at the forts.

Rates still varied depending on the location of the forts and the year. On average, a laundress washed for nineteen-and-a-half men and received a predetermined wage. In 1812, at Fort Wayne, laundresses charged twenty-five cents for washing a dozen items, if she provided the soap. If the soldier provided the soap, the rate dropped to fourteen cents a dozen.

At Fort Crawford, Wisconsin, the going rate in 1851 was fifty cents a week for two shirts, two pairs of underdrawers, and two pairs of socks. In addition, the laundress washed overcoats and blankets for twelve-and-a-half cents each, which later rose to twenty-five cents each.

Several forts set a flat rate per month, rather than asking the laundress to charge by the item. At Fort Ridgely, Minnesota, the laundresses were paid seventy-five cents a month per enlisted man. At Camp Nichols, on the Oklahoma-New Mexico border, laundresses received one dollar per month, per man. Fort Boise, Idaho, laundresses earned two dollars per month, per man.

At the frontier forts some of earlier conventions still held true. Laundresses were restricted by the rates established by the post council. They could be relieved of their duties if they charged more or otherwise cheated the men. They were responsible for any item damaged or lost while in their possession. Refusing to wash an item was not an option. Not following the rules led to dismissal of duties and the possibility of being barred from the military post altogether.

The laundresses' pay was deducted from the enlisted men's pay before the men ever received it. Otherwise, the laundresses might never have been paid. Sometimes months passed between the paymaster's visits to the posts and both soldiers, and therefore laundresses, might go for some time without being paid. Long waits between pay meant they received large sums of money when they finally were paid. This gave laundresses an opportunity to stock up on food and supplies at the commissary and the sutler's store and to pay off debts at both places. The women had to be skilled at budgeting to make ends meet until the next erratic arrival of pay.

Laundresses had the option to earn extra money by washing for officers. The post council also determined the fees for this service.

Rates ranged from piecework at one dollar per dozen to a flat three to five dollars a month. Officers were responsible for paying laundresses directly. More than one laundress had to have a commanding officer intervene so she could collect her pay from an officer.

Occasionally paymasters went beyond their duties to see that a laundress was paid her full due. Margaret Eichler was a laundress with the Fourth Cavalry Band at Fort Hays, Kansas. A Sergeant Allen, in the band, died, owing Mrs. Eichler three dollars and fifty cents for laundry services. The paymaster paid Mrs. Eichler with proceeds from Sergeant Allen's remaining wages.

Laundresses could go on strike and did so at Camp McDowell, Arizona, in 1872. Though little is known about the small rebellion, the laundresses apparently refused to wash officers' clothing. The women were not allowed to draw rations for the duration of the strike. This raises some questions since a laundress's assignment entailed washing the clothing of enlisted men only. Officers' laundry was outside of their duties, though they often completed it through special arrangements. One wonders how the commander justified withholding laundresses' rations for not completing a task that was discretionary.

Enterprising laundresses sometimes made extra money baking pies and selling them to the men. These entrepreneurial ventures seldom withstood a closer inspection. The fruit and supplies were often quietly appropriated from army supplies without a formal arrangement. Some laundresses sold milk, cream, and butter from a family cow. At Fort Laramie, Wyoming, in 1868, sixteen cows, owned by both officers and enlisted families, grazed on the grounds.

At Fort Boise, Idaho, in 1866, the military set rates for various kinds of mending the laundresses might perform in addition to routine washing of clothing. Replacing buttons brought the laundress from one cent to three cents per button, based on size. She received nine cents for repairing underdrawers and twelve cents for mending a vest. Greatcoats cost thirty-seven and one-half cents to have repaired. Laundresses could also charge for alterations with the price depending on the garment and the work done. One yard of muslin thread was priced at twenty cents.

Laundresses and enlisted personnel also owned horses, mules, or donkeys. Occasionally, the military found it necessary to limit, or in some way control, the ownership of animals. At one point during the Mexican War, non-commissioned personnel received orders to sell their equines. This order came as a result of various outrages and crimes committed against the Mexican citizens of Monterey, California, and also to their property. The army felt it necessary to limit the use and possession of riding animals. If the non-commissioned personnel did not sell, give away, or dispose of their animals in some manner, the army did it for them and kept any proceeds for the benefit of the post hospital.

The wages afforded the laundresses, combined with that of an enlisted man husband, provided a decent life for her family. The most dependable benefit was a ration of food, but other benefits existed, some more above-board than others.

3. IRON OUT THE WRINKLES: *Bibliographical Notes*

Susie King Taylor's *Reminiscences of My Life in Camp with the 33d United States Colored Troops Late 1st S. C. Volunteers* was an invaluable source. Several Internet sources have information on the Dabneys, but I found *Prologue* the newsletter of the National Archives, February 11, 2001, most helpful.

Other references for this chapter were: *Life of a Soldier on the Western Frontier* by Jeremy Agnew; *Glittering Misery: Dependents of the Indian Fighting Army* by Patricia Y. Stallard; *Army Wives on the American Frontier: Living by the Bugles* by Anne Burner Eales; *The Story of the Mexican War* by Robert S. Henry; and *Freedom's Journey: African and American Voices of the Civil War* by Donald Yacovone.

Magazine articles I once again relied on included: "The Forgotten Women of the Frontier," in *History of the West*, by S. Hansen;

"Fort Laramie: Part 5 Life of the Soldier." by David Lavender in *U.S. History*; and the important "Army Laundresses: Ladies of the 'Soap Suds Row,'" by Miller J. Stewart in *Nebraska History*. I also referenced *Historical Blotter Notes for the Post History Camp Brown, Wyoming Territory* by Dr. T. G. Maghee. Virginia Mescher's *Tubs and Duds: Civil War Laundresses in the Field, Camp, and Hospital* provided the information on rates for alterations and repairs.

A *New York Times*, opinion page article "The Nashville Experiment" by William Moss Wilson, provided information on the military hospitals at Nashville

My personal research took place at the Kansas forts—Fort Hays, Fort Larned, and Fort Riley—and in North Dakota at Fort Buford and Fort Abraham Lincoln.

4. Suds Row

AT FORT LARAMIE, a laundress was assigned living quarters in a barn. Her roommate was a cow. This was not a pleasant situation. A living area was partitioned off in the barn to provide quarters for the laundress and, presumably, her family. Unfortunately, the wall was just that, a partition, and did not go up to the ceiling or all the way down to the floor. Air circulated between the two areas and, again presumably, so did the cow's bedding and waste. The stench, flies, and humidity in the summer made the quarters unbearable. The quarters would have been very difficult to heat in the winter, although the cow provided a certain amount of body heat. Eventually, the bovine roommate, and everything else associated with living in a barn, led the post surgeon to declare this an unhealthy living situation.

———◈———

At Wyoming's Fort Phil Kearny, all but one of the four or five laundresses, were married to enlisted men. They were provided housing in ten-by-twelve-foot pole buildings with dirt roofs. However, one laundress had a different housing arrangement. An officer had a partition built in his quarters, and the laundress slept behind this partition.

Susan Fitsgerald, also known as Black Susan, was a laundress for Company H, Eighteenth U.S. Infantry. She owned a primitive "washing machine" and also had purchased a cow. Fitsgerald was known for her ability to make excellent sausage out of almost any kind of meat. She was also censured for making and selling pies to the soldiers. The pies cost fifty cents and were most likely made with supplies from the quartermaster stores. Some accounts also have her selling whiskey to the enlisted men and running a brothel. She received a hearing about her behavior where her promiscuous reputation was acknowledged. This resulted in a warning, but she continued to work at the post.

Fitsgerald had strong ties to Captain Tenador Ten Eyck. He hired her as a servant in the spring of 1866 when he was stationed in Nebraska. She followed him throughout the West during his military career. Records and diaries show that Ten Eyck made six moves between forts during a six-month span from July 1867 to January 1868. Ten Eyck shared his modified quarters at Fort Phil Kearny with Fitsgerald. One might assume that similar arrangements were made at the other forts.

Black Susan was illiterate, as most laundresses and enlisted men were at the time. Ten Eyck handled all of her monetary accounts and wrote letters to her family on her behalf. At one point, Ten Eyck sent his wife twenty dollars to buy his laundress a wig, though one cannot determine if Ten Eyck or Black Susan provided the payment.

Both Ten Eyck and, presumably, Susan Fitsgerald were at Fort Phil Kearny during of the Fetterman Battle when the entire command of Captain William Fetterman fell to combined tribal forces. Ten Eyck discovered the bodies of Fetterman and his men when he was ordered to reinforce Fetterman.

In 1868, Ten Eyck took leave and went home to Chicago. Fitsgerald accompanied him, and then went on to her home and family in Tennessee. Ten Eyck held $220 in safekeeping for her while she traveled. She returned a week later with her son and a niece. Ten Eyck wrote a letter to the principal of the Oberlin Academy, requesting Fitsgerald's sixteen-year-old son be admitted to the school. (Ten Eyck's diary indicates the boy may have been named George.) While there are no records to indicate George was admitted to Oberlin Academy, Ten Eyck did provide him room and board while he attended school in Chicago.

Black Susan traveled to Omaha in December of 1868. Ten Eyck helped her purchase a ticket and paid for some furniture. That was the last known account of her activities.

⟺◈⟹

Housing, or "quarters" in military jargon, was designated as a benefit afforded laundresses, and while Black Susan Fitsgerald had special accommodations, most laundresses did not. Housing was a requirement, but the quality or details were not specified. It varied from post to post and even varied on the same post over the years. Although some forts provided decent housing, often the quarters were described as hovels.

The location of laundress quarters was an issue. "Suds Row" was often located near the privies, behind the stables, or near the latrine outlets that drained into the river. The odors and pests were unpleasant at best. Examples are many.

Laundresses at Camp Verde, Texas, lived in perhaps the most unique of all Suds Row housing. In 1846, a large one-hundred-foot by twenty-foot structure was built as a barn for camels imported from Africa. By 1875, after the experiment with camels ran its course and the barn was no longer needed for camels, the post divided it into offices, the commissary, and three sets of laundress quarters.

In 1870, Austin, Texas, laundresses, like many others, lived in wall tents. Each tent provided a home for the laundress and her often fairly large family. A laundress had to find a place in the tent for everything she and her family owned, from furniture to smaller household items, and it made for crowded living. Single laundresses lived in tents, but presumably they did not have as many possessions. All the laundresses shared another tent as a kitchen.

Fort Abraham Lincoln, North Dakota, also housed laundresses in tents in 1873. These army issued tents were the same ones the men used, usually framed with wood and often having a canvas or wooden floor. Here the laundress tents were located close to the stables.

Tent living was fine in summer, but challenging during winter, particularly in the West, with high winds and bitter cold temperatures.

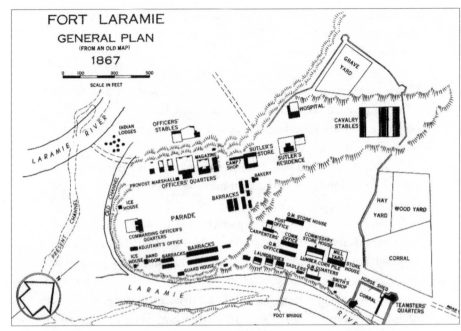

At Fort Laramie in 1876, the laundresses' quarters were along the river near the footbridge. (National Park Service, Fort Laramie National Historic Site)

Some posts provided assistance to help laundresses bank up soil and hay around the tents for warmth. Some accounts describe wash water being poured over the tent canvas to provide insulation as it froze.

A laundress described one method of heating a tent in the winter. She put a bit of soil in the bottom of a two-gallon iron pan, then filled it almost full with hot coals, and put another pan over the top. She wrote that this system kept the tent well heated through the night.

If the laundress had her own cook stove, she moved it into the tent in the winter, rather than leaving it outside where she'd used it during the summer. This presented its own set of problems. If the tent frame failed under the weight of excess snow and the tent canvas came in contact with the hot stove or stovepipe, the tent could catch on fire.

Because tent entrances usually fastened closed with ties, residents faced an ongoing challenge with drafts and snow blowing into the tent. Water buckets and food froze. Women took their sourdough starter to bed with them in an attempt to keep the culture from freezing. However, wall tents provided better shelter than other tents.

Ringold Barracks, Texas, also provided tents for the laundresses, but they were more primitive than wall tents. From 1870 to 1874, the ladies and their families were housed in tents made from boards, barrel staves, and gunnysacks. These tents were located directly behind the company barracks. A quite visible location, Suds Row there was an eyesore on an otherwise nice-looking garrison. Eventually, the post surgeon decided that because of lighting and ventilation issues and overcrowding, the housing arrangements were unhealthy and should be changed.

Charles N. Loynes described tent living at Fort Keogh, Montana, during the fall and winter of 1877–1878. His mother was one of two laundresses for Troop E. Laundresses and their soldier husbands were issued two ten-by-fourteen-foot wall tents. The occupants set them up, one in front of the other, and covered them with a large, government-issue tarp. The families lived in their tents until the following spring when houses were built for enlisted men and their wives. Loynes described the tents as being comfortable.

Before 1874, Fort Sill, Oklahoma, laundresses lived in what could, at best, be called hovels: huts, old tents, dugouts, and picket houses. Their Suds Row was located east of the sewer outlets.

At Fort Buford, North Dakota, in 1874, laundresses lived in a group of seven buildings. Dubbed "Camp Town," this housing was approximately 500 feet from the Missouri River.

At Fort Sidney, Nebraska, in 1872, housing was quite posh compared to other places. The laundress quarters were 71-foot-by-140-foot cement and stone buildings with shingled roofs. Each building housed three families. The 713-square-foot apartments worked well if the families were not too large. Presumably, the apartments were comparable with other frontier apartments when it came to light, ventilation, and heat.

However, that changed greatly a scant seventeen-years later. Captain C. S. Black noted that diphtheria, a respiratory illness, was rampant on Fort Sidney's Suds Row. The buildings were falling apart, with obvious decay, and overcrowded with too many occupants. Doctor Black declared the sanitary conditions poisonous and recommended that the laundresses and their families be moved to a healthier area.

Until 1875, Fort Dodge, Kansas, laundresses and their families were housed in dugouts or sod buildings along the river. Dugout living left much to be desired, with the dwellings having one or two rooms at best, with dirt floors and sometimes dirt walls. Logs sometimes shored up walls and roofs. The interiors were dark. In some cases, canvas covered the interior walls and ceiling, which provided a perfect hiding place and playground for packrats and mice, along with the occasional snake. Dugouts invited any number of insects, spiders, and other wildlife to take up housing with the families. In addition, the occupants suffered miserably during rainstorms.

In 1875, the military constructed new quarters for the laundresses at Fort Dodge. Four duplexes provided homes for eight families. The buildings were of board and batten construction, with two rooms per unit.

At Camp McDowell, Arizona, married enlisted men and their wives lived in adobe huts covered with brush. The post surgeon declared them unfit as living quarters. The housing for laundresses at Fort Yuma, California, was of similar construction.

In 1878, men at Fort Keogh, Montana, built log houses for laundresses and their families, as well as other married enlisted soldiers. The houses were fifty feet apart, and each house had a backyard of one hundred feet. Approximately sixty-five of these houses lined the street, which was approximately sixty-five-feet wide. This part

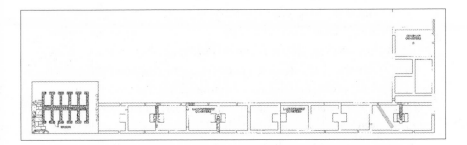

At Fort Union, New Mexico, the laundress quarters were located in the same building as the prison and the company quarters. There seems to be eight or nine rooms for laundresses. (National Park Service, Fort Union National Historic Site)

of the fort was known as Tub Town or Sudsville, as many of the residents were laundresses.

In the late 1880s, Fort Robinson, Nebraska, housed laundresses in an apartment building. The 144-foot-by-35-foot building was divided into twelve apartments, giving each family 420 square feet of living space, plus a kitchen that was added on at the back of each apartment. While adequate in size, these apartments did not allow enough light or ventilation, and they were falling apart. This, along with the residents' habit of tossing wastewater and food slops out the door plus the chicken coops and privies located close by the backdoor, led to very unsanitary situations.

Waste disposal caused problems at other forts, too. Cantonment Missouri, which later became Fort Atkinson, Nebraska, had such bad sanitation problems that officials issued orders banning reckless disposal of waste. At many forts, laundresses dumped wash water anywhere it was convenient, making a constant, muddy mess. In winter, freezing and thawing compounded the problem. In the summer, mosquitoes and other insects gravitated to the swampy ground. Numerous children, chickens, and dogs added to the unsanitary conditions surrounding the laundress quarters. At Fort

Laramie, the commander ordered a fence constructed around Suds Row to keep the mayhem contained.

At times, laundresses and other army women must have questioned their safety, living in such poor makeshift housing. Alice Baldwin, wife of Lieutenant Frank Baldwin, described the winter of 1867 at Fort Harker, Kansas. Although Mrs. Baldwin was an officer's wife, the laundresses would have experienced similar conditions. Mrs. Baldwin described the winter as exceptionally cold. Wolves thrived that winter and often came on post. The pack howled, fought, and chewed and scratched at cabin doors. Scraps of food or trash tossed in the yard encouraged the animals and were quickly devoured after dark.

On the other hand, not all laundresses lived in squalor; some of the housing was quite nice. At Fort Meade, South Dakota, the army provided single-family houses for laundresses and their families. The dwellings were conveniently located on Bear Butte Creek, with enough housing for thirteen laundresses.

Elizabeth Custer, writing about the quarters at Fort Abraham Lincoln, North Dakota, said laundresses were fortunate to get little cabins at the post. The laundress quarters were located beyond the massive stable area, home to up to six-hundred horses. Mrs. Custer described Suds Row as identifiable by the swinging clotheslines.

Jefferson Barracks, Missouri, provided decent housing for their laundresses. They, and their families, occupied a long building divided into apartments. Each family had a 380-square-foot area partitioned into two rooms. Cooking and washing facilities were provided in the basement and were apparently common areas. Two smaller buildings nearby also provided housing.

At Fort Schuyler, New York, married soldiers and their families occupied a one-story building divided into twelve sets of quarters, each with two rooms.

By 1875, the women at Fort Laramie were provided better housing. They occupied deserted cavalry barracks, located across the Laramie River from the main part of the fort.

The army had a custom called "ranking out." When a superior ranking officer arrived on post, he could move into the housing offered him, or he could bump any officer his junior and take over that housing. This junior officer could then take over the housing of an officer his junior, and so on, until no more homes remained available. Ranking out did not usually apply to laundresses, but it happened in at least one instance.

At Fort Union, New Mexico, on May 16, 1873, the post quartermaster ordered that Mrs. Ramis, laundress for Troop L, Eighth Cavalry, be moved from her quarters so the quarters could be assigned to another laundress, Mrs. Montgomery, laundress for Company C, Fifteenth Infantry. The post commander, Captain H. A. Ellis, was an officer in the Fifteenth Infantry. No reason was given for the move, but by moving Mrs. Ramis from room fourteen to room thirteen, Mrs. Montgomery procured two rooms, fourteen and fifteen. Ellis may have given preferential treatment to his own company laundress over the other laundress, an unofficial form of ranking out.

For the most part, budgetary restraints governed the quality of laundresses' housing. However, the housing was comparable to that of married enlisted men. Some soldiers used their own money to provide better housing for their families and because the laundress brought in an income, laundress families were sometimes able to improve their housing over families that did not have two incomes. Even so, home improvement opportunities are limited when a house is patched together from barrel staves and burlap. The post surgeons and commanding officers played a major role in launching both official and unofficial initiatives to provide laundresses with decent living quarters.

4. SUDS ROW: *Bibliographical Notes*

I learned much about laundress dwellings from *Glittering Misery: Dependents of the Indian Fighting Army* by Patricia Y. Stallard; *Boots and Saddles: Or Life in Dakota with General Custer* by Elizabeth Bacon Custer; *Forts of the American Frontier 1820-91: The Southern Plains and Southwest* by Ron Field; *The Gentle Tamers* by Dee Brown; and *Daughters of Joy, Sisters of Misery: Prostitutes in the American West, 1865–90* by Anne M. Butler.

I also referred to articles "Village Constructions: U. S. Army Forts on the Plains, 1848 -1890" by A. K. Hoagland; "Army Laundresses: Ladies of the 'Soap Suds Row'" by Miller J. Stewart; "The Forgotten Women of the Frontier" by S. Hansen; "Medical History, Extract from Sanitary Report, April 30, 1881" by Carlos Carvallo; "Medical Report, Fort Shuler, 1868-1869" by Assistant Surgeon C. B. White; "Fort Union and the Frontier Army in the Southwest: A Historic Resource Study Fort Union National Monument Fort Union, New Mexico" by Leo E. Oliva; and "Fort Union National Monument: Part 2, The Civil War Era" by Robert Utley.

My personal research included visits to Fort Buford, Fort Totten, and Fort Abraham Lincoln in North Dakota; Fort Meade, South Dakota; Fort Harker, Kansas; Fort Union, New Mexico; Fort Robinson, Nebraska; and Fort Laramie, Wyoming.

FAMILY LIFE AND RESPONSIBILITIES

5. The Baby and the Bathwater

THE MILITARY to a very formal hierarchy based on rank, and this structure extends to social relationships and to wives and families. An incident of cohabitation blurred the lines of the military hierarchy system at Fort Mason, Texas, in 1876. First Lieutenant Charles Field, an officer, and a laundress found a strong attraction for each other. Eventually, they lived openly as man and wife. To further complicate the matter, the laundress had a husband in Saint Louis. The army in the East would have never tolerated this behavior; however, it was overlooked on the western frontier. Even more surprisingly, the wife of the commanding officer, Albert Sidney Johnson, not only accepted the relationship, she continued to associate with Field, and presumably, his acting wife.

⋙◈⋘

Chances are that a single woman hired as a laundress married quickly after taking the job. In the general population, men outnumbered women, particularly in the frontier west, and, of course, in military camps, the shortage of women was extreme. Soldiers also saw a laundress-wife as a good investment, as she made more in one month than did an unmarried private. Not until a man earned the rank of First Sergeant did the pay become almost equal. The food a wife cooked was most likely better than that served in the barracks dining room. Marriage included the traditional benefit of female companionship and the associated bonuses.

Frontier army censuses show that the majority of officers were married, while the majority of enlisted men were not. In 1870, at

73

Fort Larned, Kansas, three of ninety-four enlisted men were married, while four of six officers had wives. In 1880, at Fort Sisseton, South Dakota, only six percent of the enlisted men were married, while all of the officers were married. At Fort D. A. Russell, Wyoming, in 1880, almost half the officers were married, while almost none of enlisted men had wives.

Marriage on the frontier often fell more into the realm of common law rather than that of a signed and sealed traditional marriage. Clergymen were uncommon. Circuit riders visited a town or outpost only once every few months. Sometimes years passed between visits. A couple wanting to marry declared, in front of witnesses, that they were married. They took up housekeeping together. When the circuit rider came around, he formalized the union, with the date of the marriage officially beginning at the original declaration. This legitimized children born before the formalization. If for some reason, the marriage did not work out before the circuit rider came around, a couple could easily separate and go on like it never happened.

The military regulations concerning married men, wives, and families varied over time, depending upon the situations and the need for soldiers and nurses, cooks, and laundresses. At times, a lottery determined how many and which women would be allowed to accompany troops.

Generally, the army discouraged soldiers from marrying. Often prior to enlistment, men had to declare their marital status and whether they had dependent children. Sometimes regulations limited the number of married enlisted men; other times an officer made an informal decision about whether the soldier was valuable enough to justify the inconvenience of his dependents.

Government regulations of 1863 based the allowable number of married men on the need for laundresses. Each company needed three or four laundresses, so was allowed three or four married men. If an enlisted soldier wished to marry, he had to ask his company commander for permission. In order to marry, the future wife either

This Civil War photo, showing a family and laundry, is identified as "Tent life of the 31 Pennsylvania Infantry, 1861." It may have been a promotional photo for the war effort. (Library of Congress)

had to be already employed as a laundress or a laundress position had to be open for her. If the commanding officer gave permission, the enlisted soldier could assume the role of a married man. Often, the captain or another officer officiated at a marriage. The validity of the union in these cases was questionable, but then usually no one inquired.

Sometimes, married couples joined the army together as a package; he as a soldier, she as a laundress. One German immigrant enlisted after having his life savings stolen. His oldest sons enlisted as privates, while his two younger sons became members of the regimental band as a drummer and a fifer. His wife and some younger daughters enlisted as laundresses while the remainder of the children worked as cooks' helpers.

Sometimes determining who was married to whom could become confusing, especially when several men seemed to be married to the same woman. Such was the case at Fort Stockton, Texas. The post surgeon noted that only four enlisted men apparently lived, on a regular basis, with their wives. Most of the other "married" soldiers lived with women they called their wives, but sometimes three or four men identified the same woman as his wife.

The doctor also commented on the low birthrate compared to the number of women living with various men. Only twelve children of enlisted men lived at the post. Indeed, one might assume that a woman who had several husbands would have multiple children. One can only assume that an effective method of birth control was practiced among the laundresses of Fort Stockton. Nationwide the contraceptive industry flourished from 1844-1873 with condoms, intrauterine devices, vaginal sponges, diaphragms, and cervical caps readily available, though perhaps not at isolated outposts. Many home remedies for birth control existed, some more effective than others.

However, that low birth rate statistic must have been localized to Fort Stockton. Husband or no husband, many laundresses had children. The Fort D. A. Russell, Wyoming, 1870 census showed twenty-four laundresses lived at the post. Uncharacteristically, only five of these women were married. Of the remaining nineteen unmarried women, seventeen had children. These seventeen women ranged in age from seventeen to forty-four years old. The two childless laundresses were sixteen and twenty-three years of age.

Children did not always arrive at the most convenient time. Mrs. Lydia B. Bacon wrote in her 1811–1812 journal that one of the soldier's wives, Mrs. Weir, delivered a baby daughter during a September night in a tent on the banks of the Wabash.

Elizabeth Custer tells the story of a blizzard that swept in suddenly on North Dakota. The general ordered the soldiers to break camp, and the men and horses to move to Yankton to seek shelter. The laundresses and a handful of officers and soldiers remained behind. During this time, a new baby came into the world, again, sheltered only by a tent.

While birth control methods were available, they were not always effective. Margaret Littlejohn, a laundress with Company I, Sixth U.S. Infantry, died on October 5, 1878, at Fort Buford, North Dakota. While her death was listed publicly as complications from a miscarriage, official records indicate she died of an abortion. It is not apparent whether the two terms were used interchangeably or if her death was the result of an unofficial surgical procedure gone wrong.

All laundresses were at a risk of unwanted sexual exploitation by officers and others. However, black laundresses seemed a special target for victimization because of the holdover mindset of slave culture. Consensual relationships between white soldiers and black laundresses were considered taboo. Some black laundresses found lovers among the white soldiers and, in keeping with the times, these relationships were usually not publicly acknowledged.

Childcare fell mostly to the women, whether or not men were available. Older children helped raise the younger ones. Children, when not in school, spent much of their day on their own in play or exploration and had chores they were expected to do.

⋘◈⋙

Women sewed their own clothes, as well as their children's clothing. They also made non-military clothing for their husbands and may have tailored uniforms both for their husbands and for other soldiers. This was most often done by hand. From the mid-1800s on, sewing machines were available, however, laundresses on the western frontier used few. They were relatively expensive and cumbersome, becoming one more item to transport and store in an already crowded home.

Because laundresses worked at difficult, dirty jobs, their dresses were simpler in design and were made of more practical, less expensive fabrics than those worn by officers' wives. Styles also varied over time. On the frontier, styles were probably three to five years behind those of the more fashionable East.

Popular fabrics of the 1870s included gingham, calicos, denim, wool, flannel, and cotton. The colors tended to be dark: indigoes, leaf shades, and browns, with complementary colors only used for flounces, bows, and adornments. Decorations on garments had little place on the workingwoman's outfit, but were added to dresses worn to social events.

Laundresses, like other women, wore several layers of clothing. They started with a chemise and drawers. The chemise was a lightweight cotton, pullover undershirt, with a hem well below the waist. The drawers were long, from waist to below the knee. They were called split drawers, because the seams were not sewn shut. The drawers fastened only at the waist and ankle.

The next layer consisted of a corset and a corset cover. The laundress wore a working corset. This item was shorter than a normal corset, allowing her more flexibility and movement. A short-sleeved, fitted shirt that buttoned or otherwise fastened down the front covered the corset. This garment was also made of cotton fabric.

The women wore black cotton or wool stockings, often of their own making. Garters held up the stockings. They wore at least two petticoats. These were cotton in the summer and warmer flannel in the winter.

Finally, a laundress wore a serviceable dress, or a skirt and blouse, constructed of any of the fabrics listed. The lighter fabrics saw service in the summer, the heavier fabrics in the winter.

An apron helped keep her dress cleaner for a longer period, and a bonnet shielded her eyes and face from the sun. Her footwear consisted of lace-up work boots, black in color.

A knitted or crocheted shawl provided cover in the summer. Winter was another story. Women layered clothing, from underwear and socks on out. Coats, hats, and gloves, made of wool, buffalo, or other furs and hides provided protection from the harsh elements.

⋘◈⋙

Education was not a priority to most laundresses and their families. At Fort Laramie, school was held during the winter months, if there

Julia Gill Schnyder, born in Ireland, arrived at Fort Laramie in 1864 as a laundress with the Eleventh Ohio Cavalry, accompanied by her sister Margaret Litsinger, also a laundress. Within the year, she married Sergeant Leodegar Schnyder and may have then retired as a laundress. They had three children and remained at Fort Laramie until 1886. She was affectionately known as "Cross-eyed Julia." This photo was taken in her later years. She died in Nebraska in 1911. (National Park Service, Fort Laramie National Historic Site)

were enough children. The children of enlisted men, and those of the quartermaster's civilian employees were required to attend, while officers' children were invited. In 1877, records show that twenty children attended the Fort Laramie school for six hours a day. Of the fourteen girls and six boys, twelve were children of enlisted men, while no officers' children attended that year. Students were between the ages of five and eleven.

Dog license fees funded the school supplies at Fort Laramie. The fort was overpopulated with canines, and in exasperation, commanding officers ordered that all canines be registered and licensed. It cost twice as much to license a female dog as a male. Money from this fund was used to purchase pens, crayons, and paper. In 1878, twenty-five-dollars worth of textbooks covering spelling, reading, and penmanship were also purchased.

Some forts offered schooling for enlisted men who wanted to learn reading, writing, basic arithmetic, and some geography. The enlisted men attended school in the evenings. Soldiers were usually assigned as teachers.

At Fort Dodge, Kansas, Private John F. Guernsey taught nineteen children in 1869. These included seven children of enlisted men, seven children of civilian employees, and five children of officers. Guernsey also taught twenty-six enlisted men. Guernsey apparently left Fort Dodge later that year, as school could not be held due to lack of an instructor.

⊰⊹⊱

Hygiene was not a high priority at frontier forts. Water was a precious commodity and usually had to be hauled from wells or rivers in buckets. Fort Harker, Kansas, got its water from two nearby springs. Water reached the fort via wooden pipes and then was stored in holding tanks. Throughout the day, water details filled barrels around the various quarters.

The priorities for water use were well established: drinking, cooking, laundry, and cleaning. There was little left over. Many forts did not have bathing facilities until later in their operation.

Although enlisted men were discouraged from marriage, Private Patrick Cloonan and Bridget Molloy married on August 3, 1873, in Fort Union, New Mexico. Both had immigrated from Ireland. She may have come West as a servant for an officer's family. After their marriage, she served as laundress until they were transferred in 1876. (National Park Service, Fort Union National Historic Site)

Bathing in the out-of-doors was impractical for the laundresses because of privacy issues. In cold months, the water froze, making any thought of outdoor bathing impossible. In warmer weather, laundresses used their tubs for bathing in their homes.

Because of the lack of sanitation, personal and otherwise, disease and health problems were an issue in the garrisons. This was often problematic, as doctor availability varied widely. Post surgeons and hospitals were available at some larger posts, especially in the later years. Civilian doctors and occasionally civilian veterinarians provided medical care. At other posts, there was no formal medical care. However, sometimes laundresses assumed the role of health care provider. Many were skilled midwives and delivered babies, not only for enlisted men's wives, but also for officers' wives. Some laundresses had knowledge of herbal medicine and other diverse healing knowledge.

Cholera, dysentery, venereal disease, and other illnesses were common among the adults at the forts. In 1867, cholera, contracted from an infected water supply, swept through Kansas and the surrounding states. It hit Fort Hays on July 11, lasting through August. Both soldiers and civilians were affected; thirty-six soldiers died.

Children also contracted cholera and dysentery, as well as diphtheria, typhoid, tetanus, and scarlet fever. Common childhood illnesses like measles, mumps, and whooping cough, practically eliminated today, were serious and even deadly. Stillborn babies were a reality.

Accidents of all kinds were common, and with access to only primitive medical treatment, the impacts were serious and recovery was slow or impossible.

Life and death were harsh realities in army camps and isolated frontier forts, and laundresses participated in the full range. In spite of lacking formal education, many laundresses acquired the knowledge and resources they needed to face the challenges that came their way—whether it be doing laundry, birthing and raising children in primitive conditions, handling first-aid emergencies, providing companionship and sex to soldiers, or preparing bodies for burial and consoling the bereaved. Laundresses were often the only women available to take on roles that have traditionally fallen to the feminine gender, and they did what they could.

5. THE BABY AND THE BATHWATER:
Bibliographical Notes

I used these primary resources for this chapter: *Life of a Soldier on the Western Frontier* by Jeremy Agnew; *Army Wives on the American Frontier: Living by the Bugles* by Anne Burner Eales; *The Gentle Tamers* by Dee Brown; *Daughters of Joy, Sisters of Misery: Prostitutes in the American West* by Anne M. Butler; *Glittering Misery: Dependents of the Indian Fighting Army* by Patricia Y. Stallard; *The History of Underclothes* by C. Willet and Phyllis Cunnington; *Victorian Working Women* by M. Hiley; *American Dress Pattern Catalogs, 1873–1909*, N. Bryk, Editor; *Victorian Costume for Ladies 1860 to 1900* by L. Setnik; *The Story of the Mexican War* by Robert S. Henry; *Violent Land: Single Men and Social Disorder from the Frontier to the Inner City* by David T. Courtwright; *Cathy Williams: From Slave to Female Buffalo Soldier* by Philip T. Tucker; *Army of Manifest Destiny: The American Soldier in the Mexican War, 1846–1848* by James M. McCaffrey; and *Boots and Saddles; or Life in Dakota with General Custer* by Elizabeth Bacon Custer. *Fort Point: Fort Point National Historic Site, Presidio of California*, Volume 2, Issue 2, provided information about laundresses at that post.

Other resources included: "Common Law Marriage" by J. Thomas, "The Roles Women Played in the War of 1812," M. Crawford, Editor; "Fort Laramie: Part 5 Life of a Soldier" by David Lavender; "Village Constructions: U. S. Army Forts on the Plains, 1848–1890" by A. K. Hoagland; "Army Laundresses: Ladies of the

'Soap Suds Row'" by Miller J. Stewart; and "Common Law Marriage" by D.K. Nix. I also accessed a web page from Fort Concho, Texas, "The Army Laundress."

I conducted personal research and site visits for this chapter primarily at Fort Buford, North Dakota, and at the Victorian Dress Museum in Rugby, North Dakota.

SOCIAL LIFE

6. On the Side

IN THE SUMMER of 1877, Emily McCorkle FitzGerald, wife of an
army doctor, discovered living in Fort Lapwai, Idaho, to be a
stark contrast to the time she and her family spent in Alaska for
her husband's previous assignment. The temperatures in Idaho av-
eraged in the high eighties and nineties during the day, dropping
down to the fifties at night. A slight breeze blew constantly. The
sunshine on the rich hills dotted with wildflowers was a vast change
from the overcast, damp coastal greenery she had grown accustomed
to in Sitka, Alaska. But Emily was never one to complain. In her
letters home to her mother, she wrote enthusiastically about the
beauty of both landscapes.

At Fort Lapwai, Idaho, when a company laundress's husband
was killed in battle with the Nez Perce, the FitzGeralds provided a
safe home for her and her children. The laundress, Mrs. Hurlburt,
was nearing the end of a pregnancy. Her quarters were located
outside the garrison, and she feared that she would not be able to
get her family to safety if the Indians attacked. Few trees covered
the area along the creek or in front of officers' row. They would not
have provided much cover in the event of an attack.

Mrs. FitzGerald felt this laundress was a very nice woman and
complimented her well-behaved children. The doctor's wife planned
to take up a monetary collection after the baby was born to send the
laundress, her new baby and children back east, where she had friends.

FitzGerald was never one to worry much about social status.
She was part of another arrangement that blurred social hierarchy

85

at Fort Lapwai. All women at the fort gathered in one home when an impending Indian attack was announced. Officers' wives and laundresses alike shared in the fear and excitement, and one officer's wife even donned her husband's gun belt.

Another account of an officer's wife who disregarded military hierarchy comes from Fanny Dunbar Corbusier in her recollections. She writes that when her second son was born in Camp Date Creek, Arizona, a laundress, Mrs. Leahy, came into her home for two weeks to help with her family and household work. Mrs. Leahy was also the mother of a new baby, only a few months old. Fanny writes that the Corbusier's new son could not take all the milk she produced so she shared it with Mrs. Leahy's baby. "He was always very hungry and pulled hard. When he was satisfied he looked very happy."

Elizabeth Custer tells a story that documents the common rigid division between officers' wives and laundresses in most camps. An old Irish laundress was looking for work as an officer's cook. She was offered a job cooking for an officer who had risen through the ranks. His wife had previously worked as a military laundress when her husband had been an enlisted man. The old Irish woman refused the job, because she had personally known the officer's wife when both worked as laundresses and apparently believed herself unable to treat her former contemporary with the respect accorded an officer's wife and a lady.

Author Michele Nacy, in *Members of the Regiment,* writes these former laundresses, newly reborn as officers' wives, were sometimes called "half-way ladies." The term was used derogatorily, indicating that the former laundresses would never be true ladies because of their lack of refinement and education. Some society-conscious officers' wives apparently believed that the army could promote a soldier from enlisted man to officer, but nobody could promote his wife from laundress to lady.

This class distinction based on rank revealed itself when a laundress testified as a witness in a trial. An officer faced a court-martial for conduct unbecoming a gentleman. In the end, the laundress's testimony was deemed worthless because of her social class, and because she, a white woman, was married to a black soldier.

⟨⟩

Fort life included dances and other social activities. However, the class division usually separated the activities into those for officers and those for lower ranking men and women. Military balls were the main form of amusement at many of posts. Laundresses mingled with servants and the wives and daughters of enlisted men at dances strictly for members of their social status. Officers and their wives had their own balls. Women were in short supply at the frontier outposts; hence, no woman ever lacked dance partners, no matter how homely or old.

Some dances were impromptu affairs, perhaps cooked up by the military band. The various companies at a post sometimes sponsored formal balls, which required preparations well in advance. This included finding a place to hold the dance, often in the barracks. At Fort Laramie, Wyoming, the barracks floors were scrubbed clean and bunks stacked away on top of each other to provide a place for dancing.

At Fort Totten, North Dakota, the post trader's store provided the space for dancing. Children, even babies, accompanied their mothers to the dances. Babies stayed in the relative quiet of the first sergeant's quarters for the duration of the festivities.

Laundresses did their best to wear their finest clothing to the dances. Fashionable clothing was hard for laundresses to acquire or to afford. Many styles did not suit the reddened skin of the hard working laundresses, but they wore them anyway. Mrs. Custer writes that her laundress, Mrs. Nash, wore a pink Tarleton striped dress and false curls in her hair to the dance.

Enlisted men's dances generally opened with a brief visit from the commanding officer and his wife, with other officers present as well. They danced one or two dances and then left the enlisted ranks to celebrate on their own, thus maintaining the military decorum.

These festive affairs often ended up in fights and other dis-
agreements, due to the amount of liquor consumed. Problems often
arose because of a jealous spouse. A Dutch-born laundress, nicknamed "Old Trooble Agin" by Elizabeth Custer, was not allowed by
her husband to dance with anyone other than him.

Occasionally, officers and their wives did intermingle with the
enlisted ranks for entire dances. One case was a Saint Patrick's Eve
dance at Fort Custer where the ladies of the fort, including the officers' wives, laundresses, and other servants, sat with the visiting
town women for the midnight supper. All reportedly had a good
time, so one might assume they found commonality.

Soldiers sometimes joined in stag dances when no women were
available as partners. A chosen man simply indicated he was playing
the role of a woman by tying a white handkerchief around his arm.

Aside from dances, music often provided additional entertainment. Band concerts and occasional glee club performances brought
the fort's occupants together.

Scholarly lectures on various topics were sometimes offered
with these probably aimed at the better-educated officers and their
families.

Theatrical performances crossed the social boundaries at the
forts. Officers, enlisted men, laundresses, civilians, and family members joined together to perform the roles, and they also provided
the audience.

At Fort Laramie and other posts, dress parades occupied Sunday
evenings, weather permitting. Most of the post's occupants came to
watch the soldiers drill in their best uniforms. The parades boosted
morale by giving all of the people at the fort a sense of pride.

Competitive baseball leagues provided entertainment at the
forts, but for the women, this meant just watching the games. Although army regulations forbade betting on the outcome, most
commanders ignored friendly wagering.

The celebration of holidays was a welcome change of routine.
Most soldiers and officers had a day off from duties, as did the

Like that of many people, much of an army laundress's social life was built around her work. Here laundresses gather at a stream to wash clothing and visit about their family, friends, and happenings. (Library of Congress)

laundresses. Holidays celebrated included New Year's Day, Washington's Birthday, Independence Day, Thanksgiving (after it became a holiday in 1863), and Christmas. Holiday celebrations varied but included parades, races (on foot, horseback, or mule), games, and parties. The holiday celebrations were a rare time when class distinctions were erased among the various groups of people. Officers and their families intermingled with enlisted ranks and civilians.

On the Fourth of July, young and old alike participated in numerous games like wheelbarrow races, sack races, and other similar activities. Horse races put to rest the question of who rode the swiftest mount, and fireworks exploded into the night.

Soldiers planned a big Independence Day celebration at Fort Riley, Kansas, in 1854, and thought it would be enhanced if whiskey and wine flowed freely. Some of the soldiers and civilian workers made secret arrangements for the delivery of 150 gallons of illicit whiskey and ten gallons of wine. A few days before the holiday, the libations were stealthily delivered to a spot near Three Mile Creek, a short distance from the fort. One of the privates in on the scheme helped unload the whiskey and could not resist sampling the brew. As the last barrel was being unloaded, a sergeant and two other soldiers appeared on the scene and threatened to spoil the plot by reporting the complicit men to officials. The tipsy private begged for mercy. The civilian supplying the liquor offered the sergeant ten dollars as an incentive to keep quiet and promised to destroy the kegs. The enterprising sergeant instead confiscated the liquor and later privately sold it for a dollar a quart. The Fourth of July was celebrated with more decorum.

Christmas was, of course, another big day in the garrisons. Christmas Eve, 1885, at Fort Leavenworth, Kansas, was celebrated by an invitation to church for both enlisted men and officers and their families. Every child at church that night received a gift box of candy and an orange.

A Christmas party at Fort Yates, North Dakota, in 1886, entertained all of the children at the post. The dance hall sported a beautiful Christmas tree. Every child on post, whether a child of officers, enlisted men, laundresses, or civilians, received treats of fruit, a toy, candy, and popcorn.

Fort Coeur d'Alene, Idaho, residents celebrated Christmas in the theatre, an abandoned barracks building. The Christmas tree was beautifully decorated with expensive gifts, purchased by the officers and their wives. These gifts went to the laundresses' children. Santa Claus appeared and distributed the many gifts.

Though the laundresses enjoyed the many social activities, life at the isolated forts could be particularly lonely for women, and the military lifestyle was difficult. Often small human kindnesses and friendships were all that made military life bearable. One military wife explained, "just a handful of people . . . afloat upon an un-charted sea of desolation, miles and miles from civilization, and the shared hardships of a bleak climate . . . and the daily perils they faced together. These were the factors that brought army pioneers closer to each other . . . than many brothers and sisters."

Civil War laundress Susie King Taylor, in her memoir, recounted the story about soldiers asking why she was so kind to them, even though they were not part of her company. She replied that they were all the same, whether part of her unit or not. They were all fighting and doing their duty, and she was not making any distinc-tions. The soldiers were grateful she had taken an interest in them and that she looked after them as best she could.

Sometimes friendships extended across the boundaries of the ranks. Alice Baldwin, wife of Lieutenant Frank Baldwin, was twenty-two-years old when she left a beautiful home in the east to travel to Fort Harker, Kansas. When the couple arrived at Fort Harker during thick snow, Allie saw no buildings, only a stovepipe emerging from a mound of snow. "Where is our house?" she asked. Imagine her despair when she learned her home was a dugout located under that snow, and, since they arrived unexpectedly, the stove had not been lit.

Mrs. Kelly, who may have worked as a laundress and was the wife of the commissary sergeant, recognized how distraught Mrs. Baldwin was and offered her comfort and friendship. Allie Baldwin wrote of Mrs. Kelly: "She was a kindly soul, and her womanly heart at once divined the loneliness and depressed feelings of the forlorn and homesick bride, and she sought . . . to console and cheer."

Martha Summerhayes, wife of Major John Summerhayes, tells of receiving comfort from a laundress when the major went out on a campaign. The laundress, named Mrs. Patten, stayed with her for two months at Fort D. A. Russell, Wyoming. The Sioux were ru-mored to be ready to attack at any moment, and Mrs. Summerhayes was fearful of being alone. She referred to Mrs. Patten as an old campaigner and was very grateful for the companionship that the Irish woman provided.

Isolation, necessity, and safety all played a role in the blurring of societal lines at military outposts. Men adhered more strictly to the military boundaries dividing officers from enlisted men. But women needed feminine companionship, and not many women were available in the outposts, so friendships sometimes sprung up between unlikely candidates.

6. ON THE SIDE: *Biographical Notes*

Emily FitzGerald's letters have been collected into a book (see complete bibliography) and proved very helpful. Martha Summerhayes's book, *Vanished Arizona,* is a wonderful first-hand account of her experiences as an army wife. Michele Nacy's book, *Members of the Regiment,* provided information on the term "half-way ladies." *Fanny Dunbar Corbusier: Recollections of Her Army Life, 1869-1908* includes the story of nursing her laundress's baby.

Other resources for this chapter include: *A Frontier Army Christmas* by Lori A. Cox-Paul and James W. Wengert; *Army Wives on the American Frontier Living by the Bugles* by Anne Burner Eales; *Boots and Saddles; or Life in Dakota with General Custer* by Elizabeth Bacon Custer; *Indian War Veterans: Memories of Army Life and Campaigns in the West, 1864–1898* by Jerome A. Greene; *My Life in Camp* by Susie King Taylor; and *Glittering Misery: Dependents of the Indian Fighting Army* by Patricia Y. Stallard.

Helpful journal articles include: "The Forgotten Women of the Frontier" by S. Hansen, and "Fort Laramie: Part 5 Life of the Soldier" by David Lavender.

I conducted on-site research including trips to Fort Lincoln and Fort Totten, North Dakota.

7. Extra Baggage

ELLEN WILLIAMS, LAUNDRESS and nurse with what was originally the Colorado Volunteer Infantry, provided one of the best descriptions of traveling with the troops.

In October of 1861, Ellen's husband, Charles, enlisted as a bugler, and she was appointed as a company laundress. Captain James Ford also signed her on as a nurse. In December, the company was mustered into service, and the Williams family traveled to Fort Garland, Colorado. They then received orders to go to Santa Fe, New Mexico. The column began what was expected to be a ten-day march in February 1862. Because of severe snowstorms and icy trails, the march took almost a month, and rations became limited. Ox-carts were to provide transportation for the women and children, but the rough terrain made riding in them impossible. Mrs. Williams had a young child and a baby. She and the child walked most of the way, and soldiers helped carry the baby. The entire unit suffered from intense cold and hunger. Mrs. Williams was concerned that the children might freeze to death in the night and made sure they slept between her and her husband.

After the company arrived in Santa Fe, they eventually marched to Fort Union, New Mexico, where they remained until early 1863. They then were ordered to return to Colorado. Mrs. Williams dreaded a repeat of their mid-winter march. However, this time the trip was comparatively easy.

In November 1863, the Williams family received orders to travel to Kansas with their company, in preparation for Civil War service. This was a cold, hard, six-week-long march. They traveled hundreds of miles across the plains, through howling winds and blowing snow. They passed many houses along the way. The women swallowed their pride and asked local residents for overnight lodging for themselves and their children, but their requests were mostly denied. Residents seemed to have little sympathy for the travelers. The soldiers did what they could to help the women, but the constant setting up camp, packing and unpacking, and sleeping outside in the bad weather were definite hardships for all.

The company arrived in Kansas City early in 1864. The regiment was merged with other Colorado troops to form Company A, Second Colorado Cavalry, and were stationed at Hickman's Mill, Missouri, for most of the year. They then received orders to fight Confederate forces heading towards Kansas City. Although most women were not allowed to accompany the troops, Mrs. Williams went because of her nursing duties. Their mission successful, the Second Colorado Cavalry was transferred to Fort Leavenworth, Kansas. On December 21, 1864, Charles Williams was mustered out, after the couple had traveled approximately one thousand miles on foot and in wagons in all kinds of weather.

⋖❖⋗

In 1846, John W. Hess enlisted in the Mormon Battalion, the only religion-based military unit ever in the United States. His wife, Emeline, signed on as a laundress so that she could accompany him. The newly formed battalion departed from Council Bluffs, Iowa, in July with orders to travel two hundred miles to Fort Leavenworth, Kansas. Hess was a teamster, driving a team of six mules pulling a supply wagon. This benefitted Emeline. The wagons were loaded to the top with all of the necessary equipment, including tents, kettles, cooking utensils, stakes, poles, and more. The women were allowed to ride in the wagons if there was room, but they had to maintain the same cramped position for long periods of time. Because Hess was in charge of loading his own wagon, he was able to arrange the load to make Emeline a bit more comfortable.

Ellen Williams, from the frontispiece of her book which was published in 1885, about 24 years after her experience as an army laundress. Her book is likely the only surviving memoir written by the wife on an enlisted man in the frontier West.

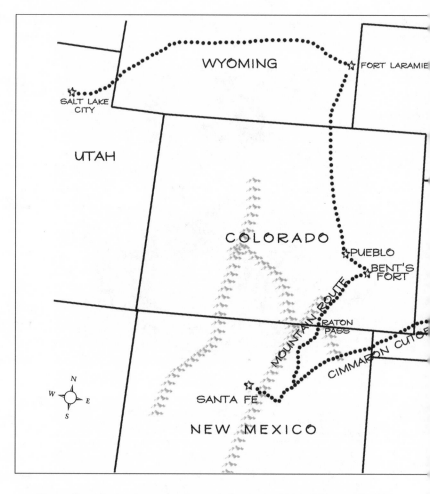

From Fort Leavenworth, the unit began a 720-mile march to
Santa Fe. Most of the battalion traveled on foot. Much of the
journey was over bleak ground, with little water or grass. Buffalo
chips provided fuel. One part of the trek involved crossing an eighty-
mile long desert with the only water available being what each man
could carry in his two-quart canteen. Many of the men collapsed
during this journey and had to be assisted by others.

After reaching Santa Fe, the battalion was ordered to go on a
forced march to California to join the fight against the Mexicans. It

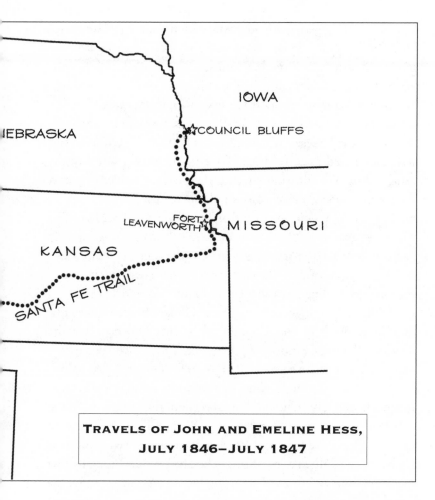

IOWA

NEBRASKA

★ COUNCIL BLUFFS

LEAVENWORTH FORT MISSOURI

KANSAS

SANTA FE TRAIL

**TRAVELS OF JOHN AND EMELINE HESS,
JULY 1846–JULY 1847**

would become the longest infantry march in history. Because the women, children, and the disabled and sick would slow the march, they were to be sent to Pueblo, Colorado. Hess did not think the trip would be safe for the dependents, so he summoned his courage and requested permission from his captain for the husbands to travel with their wives to Pueblo. His request was denied, so he resolved to go the post commander who gruffly denied his request, saying military families should expect to be separated and that he too had left his wife behind. Hess writes in his diary that he replied,

"Colonel, I suppose you left your wife with friends, while we are required to leave ours in an enemy's country in the care of sick, demoralized men." Surprisingly, permission was granted, and the men were allowed to accompany their wives.

This was a relatively short journey of approximately 280 miles, yet it proved arduous. They were dispatched with the poorest oxen and wagons and traveled with soldiers unfit for service. Once on their way, they found they had been allotted only three-quarters of the usual rations. Since they moved so slowly, they soon needed to stretch the supply by going on half rations and later on quarter rations. Upon finally reaching a supply point at Bent's Fort, the group was restocked while the captain went back to Santa Fe to collect their wages as they had not been paid in seven months. On the captain's return, they traveled on more easily to Pueblo for the winter. They built houses of cottonwood, joining them all together to form a stockade.

In April the following year, the detachment headed three hundred miles north to Fort Laramie, where they hoped to join the Mormon Pioneer Company led by Brigham Young who was traveling west looking for a permanent location for the Latter Day Saints. However, Young's group was about two weeks ahead of the detachment. The military column followed behind, finally arriving in the Salt Lake Valley about four days after Young's Pioneer Company. On July 27, 1847, John and Emeline were discharged from their service to the United States Army. They had traveled roughly two thousand miles in just one year, all by foot or wagon.

⟠

Moving the laundresses with the troops was an exercise in logistics for both the laundresses and the army. Laundresses had buckets, tubs, washboards, and many other job-related items that had to come along with the women. They often had children, along with all the paraphernalia that homes and children entail, including beds and cribs. Inspector General Randolph B. Marcy remarked, in 1875, that the baggage of four laundresses with children amounted to more than that of all the enlisted men in the company.

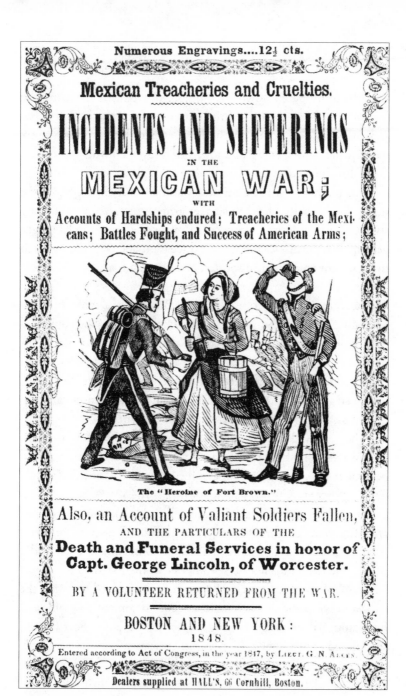

Numerous Engravings....12½ cts.

Mexican Treacheries and Cruelties.

INCIDENTS AND SUFFERINGS

IN THE

MEXICAN WAR;

WITH

Accounts of Hardships endured; Treacheries of the Mexicans; Battles Fought, and Success of American Arms;

The "Heroine of Fort Brown."

Also, an Account of Valiant Soldiers Fallen,

AND THE PARTICULARS OF THE

Death and Funeral Services in honor of Capt. George Lincoln, of Worcester.

BY A VOLUNTEER RETURNED FROM THE WAR.

BOSTON AND NEW YORK:

1848.

Entered according to Act of Congress, in the year 1847, by LIEUT. G. N. ALLEN.

Dealers supplied at HALL'S, 66 Cornhill, Boston.

"The Heroine of Fort Brown," Sarah Bourgette, was also known as "the Great Northern" because of her similarity to a steamboat bearing that name. She traveled from Florida to Mexico with the troops.

The army pared down the number of laundresses during the Indian Wars because of the difficulties in moving them. Before the Indian Wars, depending on the regiment's orders, as many as six women per 100 men were allowed to move. During the Indian Wars this changed to four laundresses per eighty men.

For many years, the laundresses and all of their baggage were transported in big, blue Studebaker army wagons, each pulled by six mules. Either four horses or four mules pulled later model freight wagons. A standard wagonload was three thousand pounds, although more weight could be transported over smooth roads.

An exception to all routine was Sarah Bourgette, a camp follower and laundress of the Seventh United States Infantry. She consorted with many men, married several husbands, and used many last names, including Bowman, Borginnis, Davis, and her maiden name, Knight. Her nicknames were many, including "Great Northern" after a steamboat noted for its size, "Great Western" as a variation on the theme, and "The Heroine of Fort Brown."

She followed the troops from Florida to the Mexico front. Before 1840, she had married a soldier named John Langwell and become a laundress. The couple joined Brigadier General Zachary Taylor's forces in Corpus Christi, Texas, in 1845.

In 1846, she remarried, this time to a soldier named Borginnis, and they were assigned to Fort Brown, Texas. This new husband was in the Second Dragoons, and Sarah worked as a cook and a nurse. She distinguished herself among women at the crossing of Arroyo Colorado in March 1846, when she offered to wade the river and whip the enemy singlehandedly if someone would lend her a stout pair of tongs. During the bombardment of Fort Brown, she refused to seek shelter with the other women but instead calmly operated the officers' mess in spite of stray shell fragments that lodged in her sunbonnet. She was noted for her bravery in battle, especially when caring for injured soldiers. Newspapers then gave Sarah the sobriquet "The Heroine of Fort Brown."

Sarah Bourgette, alaso known as both Sarah Bowman and the Great Northern among other nicknames, allegedly offered fifteen thousand dollars and the biggest leg in all of Mexico to any soldier who would marry her so she could travel with the troops to California as a laundress. (Illustration by Bob Boze Bell, *True West* magazine)

When the men moved, Sarah drove her donkey cart, loaded with supplies, to Mexico, proving she was one laundress who didn't need the army's help in moving. She was said to drive in the manner of the foulest teamster, while her six-foot-tall, voluptuous figure reminded some observers of a waterfront madam.

After her second husband was killed in combat the same year they were married, she traveled with the army into the interior of Mexico and went on to manage two hotels in the Mexican cities of Saltillo and Monterrey. She was illiterate, but fluent in spoken Spanish and English, and was an excellent manager. Sarah also acquired a variety of other male companions and later married again.

Here Sarah's story takes on the stuff of legend. She later wanted to join a band of dragoons that were headed to California, but was told she would have to be married to a soldier in order to sign on as a laundress. By this time, she was a woman of means due to her successful civilian business ventures. According to the story, she climbed on a mount and rode back and forth in front of the troops saying, "Who wants a wife with fifteen thousand dollars and the biggest leg in all of Mexico? Come on my beauties, don't speak all at once. Who is the lucky man?"

She settled on a man named Davis, who was part of E Company. Davis wanted the marriage to be performed by a minister, but the Great Northern's response was straightforward. "Bring your blanket to my tent tonight, and I will learn you to tie a knot that will satisfy you, I reckon," she reportedly said.

Alas, both the romance and her career as a laundress were short-lived. A few days later the Seventh left Chihuahua, Mexico, and ran into a party of traders from Santa Fe. After seeing one fellow bathing, Sarah was completely taken by his large size and strength. Davis was forgotten, and she took the new trader as her lover.

Following another stint in private industry in El Paso, including being the first madam in the city, she moved to Fort Yuma. She married, for at least the fourth time, to a Mexican-American War veteran named Albert J. Bowman. She cooked and cleaned for officers and opened a brothel across the street from the fort. She died on December 23, 1866, of a reported spider bite. She was buried with full military honors. When Fort Yuma closed in 1890, she was reburied at the San Francisco National Cemetery, in a private grave.

Sarah had been well respected in her own way and was described as masculine with a female heart. John Ford, a Texas Ranger, said she could whip any man, in a fair or foul fight; could shoot a pistol better than anyone; and could out-play or out-cheat any gambler. Newspaperman Braxton Bragg described her "unflagging devotion to her boys."

⸻◈⸻

Though Sarah preferred to travel by her own means, military-wife and memoirist Martha Summerhayes described a more typical line-up for a march. The main body of troops marched in the front of

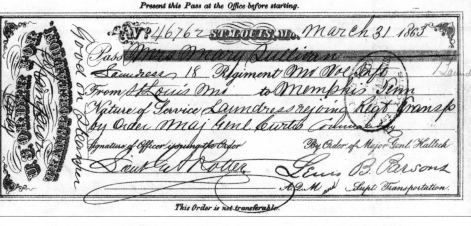

A transportation order for Mrs. Mary Sullivan, a laundress, allowing her to travel from St. Louis to Memphis to rejoin her regiment. Across the left end is written "Good on Steamer Champion Only." (Missouri History Museum, St. Louis)

the column. The ambulances came next, generally carrying officers' wives and families. The Studebaker wagons came next. The laundresses and their children either rode in these wagons or walked. A small rear guard completed the lineup. Dust rose constantly, coating everything. In addition, beef cows and other livestock might accompany the column, off to the side or bringing up the rear. The column progressed an average of ten to fifteen miles a day, making moving a long, arduous journey.

The laundresses' lives during troop movement mirrored the lives of the women who crossed the country in wagon trains. They camped out, often sharing tents with other laundresses. Little privacy existed, and they were grateful to arrive at their post.

Because of the complications of moving laundresses, they were normally left behind when the men went out on a campaign. On October 2, 1876, Company B left Camp Brown, Wyoming, for Fort Reno, a trip of approximately 210 miles. The men marched; no laundresses accompanied them.

Sometimes laundresses went partway with their companies and then were left at a military camp along the way. In 1879, laundresses of the Twenty-third Infantry were told that they would be left off at Fort Dodge if they went with the regiment. Later that day, they received orders that they would not be allowed to accompany the troops at all.

When not traveling via a march with the troops, a laundress's typical journey to an assignment might include any combination of trains, stagecoaches, and wagons.

In October 1873, fourteen laundresses were sent to Fort Riley, Kansas, by train. A laundress named Kate Gratz needed to travel from Fort Hayes, Kansas, to Fort Dodge to join her company, the Tenth Cavalry, Troop K. She traveled via railroad and stagecoach. Another pair of laundresses and two privates of the Tenth Cavalry, Troop I, were sent together to Fort Wallace, Kansas; however, their mode of travel was not recorded.

Three officers' wives and an enlisted man's wife relocated by train to Fort Bridger, Wyoming, in 1876. Young Rachel Lobach Brown, wife of Sergeant Henry Brown, was possibly a laundress. She had a seventeen-month-old baby and was extremely frightened because Custer and his men had recently been killed at the Little Big Horn. The officers' wives provided comfort and helped care for the child as they traveled.

Mrs. Mahoney, a laundress with the Ninth Infantry, Company E, needed to travel in Wyoming from Fort Laramie to Fort Fetterman, en route to Cantonment Reno. She traveled in the company of a Sergeant Scully and his laundress wife.

During the Nez Perce conflict, the army was in the process of establishing a small post near Missoula, Montana, to be called Fort Missoula. Two companies of the Seventh Infantry, officers' wives and children, and laundresses had been there for less than a month, with the men working on the construction, when they were told the Nez Perce were approaching their camp, pursued by General Oliver Howard. The men hurried to build fortifications. They cut down any brush that might provide natural cover for the Indians, built rifle pits, and piled up sacks of grain to provide the best protection that they could for the women and children. The tribe passed several miles from the fort and the military women and children were not placed in harm's way, but to military leaders it was one more example of laundresses being "extra baggage."

When the government began talks about phasing out the laundresses, transportation was one of the major topics of discussion. Several officers including Colonel Regis de Trobriand brought up the labor and expense of transporting the laundresses, however General E. O. C. Ord believed that if the laundresses were denied transportation, they would find some way to smuggle themselves, their children, and their belongings along on the marches. They wanted to be with their husbands, he said, and usually their husbands wanted their wives.

7. EXTRA BAGGAGE: *Biographical Notes*

I relied on the following resources for this chapter: *Life of a Soldier on the Western Frontier* by Jeremy Agnew; *Army Wives on the American Frontier: Living by the Bugles* by Anne Burner Eales; *The Gentle Tamers* by Dee Brown; *Boots and Saddles; or Life in Dakota with General Custer* by Elizabeth Bacon Custer; *Women of the New Mexico Frontier 1846–1912* by Cheryl J. Foote; *Three and a Half Years in the Army* by Ellen Williams; *Historical Blotter Notes for the Post History of Camp Brown, Wyoming Territory* by T. G. Maghee; and *Glittering Misery: Dependents of the Indian Fighting Army* by Patricia Y. Stallard. *Vanished Arizona*, by Martha Summerhayes, is a wonderful officer's wife memoir, which provided additional information.

The information about the laundresses of the Seventh Infantry being in the predicted path of the Nez Perce is from the firsthand account of Charles N. Loynes in Jerome A. Greene's collection *Indian War Veterans*.

Other resources include magazine articles: "Army Laundresses: Ladies of the 'Soap Suds Row'" by Miller J. Stewart and "The Roles Women Played in the War of 1812" by Helen Ferguson; and the Orson Pratt Brown website.

Cheryl J. Foote, author of *Women of the New Mexico Frontier, 1846-1912,* steered us in the right direction to find the illustration of Ellen Williams.

My on-site research took me to various forts in Kansas.

8. Dirty Laundry

MRS. NASH IS perhaps the most famous laundress of them all. Mrs. Nash, whose first name is not recorded, was nicknamed "Old Nash," and followed the Seventh Cavalry for a number of years. She had worked for Elizabeth Custer, wife of George Armstrong Custer, and earned admiration with the meticulous care she gave laundry. Mrs. Nash was of Mexican ethnicity, and like Linty, the Nebraska laundress, she was quite tall and angular. Despite her appearance, she had a tender heart and was often married to an enlisted man.

Mrs. Nash not only worked as a laundress, but she also retailored uniforms for soldiers and baked and sold pies. She managed to save a good amount of money, but her husband stole it and left her. Although she did not legally divorce Nash, she married another soldier. They went with the regiment to Dakota Territory. That husband also deserted both the army and her, again taking all of her money.

Mrs. Nash had great skill as a midwife and nurse and was highly respected by the other women at the fort, though she was reserved and a bit different. Despite her previous record with men, she decided to try one more marriage, this time to Corporal Patrick Noonan at Fort Meade, South Dakota. Unfortunately, she became gravely ill while her husband was away with his unit. When it had become apparent to her that she would not survive, Mrs. Nash pleaded with the other women at the fort to avoid fussing over her burial. She asked them to bury her as she was, without delay or any special preparations. However, when the time came, the women found this request unthinkable. They held Mrs. Nash in high esteem

The Laundress Nash story was covered by the Bismarck Tribune *in detail and picked up by East Coast newspapers. This artwork claiming to be "an authentic portrait" appeared in the* National Police Gazette.

and called her "the most popular midwife in the garrison," so they decided to honor her with a proper burial. While preparing Mrs. Nash's body for services, the other women were very surprised to find that their beloved laundress was physically a man.

When he returned to the fort, Mrs. Nash's husband was interviewed by the *Bismarck Tribune* which reported "he didn't know his wife was a man" and that they had hoped to have children. Two days later, unable to bear the harassment and grief, Corporal Noonan died when he shot himself in the stables at Fort Abraham Lincoln. He is buried at Little Bighorn Battlefield National Cemetery.

Some accounts say that the laundress had first enlisted in the army as a man and served as a freighter before finding the life of a woman and the work of a laundress more to her liking

———⊰❋⊱———

Much of what is known about laundresses comes from the journals of officers or their wives. Commanding officers also left a few records regarding laundresses, but most paperwork was kept at a company level and has not survived. Because of this, most of the laundresses who stood out enough to be written about were colorful or had a darker side. Their transgressions included running afoul of the law, running a side business of prostitution, or being a nonconformist. This is a classic example of a few individuals giving many a bad name. By comparing the number of laundresses written about in a negative manner with the total number of laundresses employed, it is easy to see that the majority must have been generally unassuming, hard-working, honest women who did not attract much attention.

Laundresses were sanctioned by the army and, therefore, had to follow army rules and regulations. Their captain decided their punishment and fate, should that become necessary. Punishments ranged from losing their whiskey ration, to losing their jobs, to being thrown off the post. The former punishment was meted out to a laundress at Cantonment Missouri (Fort Atkinson), Nebraska. She was accused of throwing out her dirty wash water in a restricted area in front of the quarters of Light Company A, Sixth Infantry. She pleaded guilty and lost her whiskey ration for ten days.

While other examples of punishment were recorded fairly frequently, oftentimes one senses that part of the story is left untold. At Fort Atkinson, Nebraska, sometime in the 1820s, an irate laundress named Hannah publicly berated the Officer of the Day, Captain Bennett Riley. This did not set well with him. He charged her with using disrespectful language, and she went before a military court that found her guilty. She was discharged from the service and kicked off the post. However, the commanding officer sympathized with her and remitted the sentence.

In her book *Boots and Saddles,* Elizabeth Custer writes of her husband's problems with laundresses. She claimed that many of the women were fighters, and the slightest infringement of their rights brought on physical and verbal battles. General Custer had to listen to both sides of the argument and issue a judgment. Occasionally, the battles involved husband and wife. He then gave them marriage counseling. The mental image of General Custer as a marriage counselor is bemusing, but not inaccurate.

Jake Tonmichel, a resident of Fort Laramie in the 1870s and 1880s, acknowledged that laundresses fought, as did soldiers and children. Fighting was part of life at the post, he said.

One laundress at another post was brought up on assault charges. The victim was her husband. She claimed she hit him with a tin cup; he claimed she used an axe. She was arrested and held in the guardhouse. Her sentence required she be drummed off the post, under the force of bayonets, in front of the soldiers. After that she and her children made their home off the post, in a cold house with little food. This was not the first problem this laundress had with military authority. Earlier, she was threatened with the extremes of death or flogging for allowing two of her children to ride in an ambulance during a march.

Mrs. Cavanaugh, a laundress at Camp McDermitt, Nevada, threatened to kill an officer in retaliation for his action against her husband. The laundress's husband, a blacksmith, had been drunk at the evening stable call, and the first lieutenant ordered the man tied up by his thumbs. Mrs. Cavanaugh took umbrage at this and threatened the officer with a huge carving knife. While Mrs. Cavanaugh's punishment, if any, is not recorded, the officer-memoirist recalling this wrote it was "the last instance of the infliction of brutal punishment upon a soldier" within his remembrance. So Mrs. Cavanaugh apparently made her point.

Another laundress, of Mexican heritage, stationed at Fort Bascom, New Mexico, in 1866, took offense at a remark a soldier made about her. The laundress told the soldier that if he said anything more about her, she would cut his tongue out. He did not heed her threat and spoke out against her again. A woman of her word, she cut off the tip of his tongue when he was sleeping off a drinking binge. Again, only the crime was reported in a memoir and not the punishment.

Both crime and results are recorded for Mrs. Julia Roach, a laundress at Fort C. F. Smith, Montana. She was married to Corporal John Doyle of Company G, Twenty-seventh Infantry. Mrs. Roach did not come west with her husband, as he had come ahead of her, trying to escape her temper. He even changed his name to Doyle. Despite his efforts, Julia tracked him down, and she joined him at the fort in 1878.

Mrs. Roach not only found it necessary to berate and disparage her husband constantly, but she also did so to any soldier that she encountered. On the morning of July 25, Corporal Doyle could take no more. He gunned down his wife at close range on the street between the company barracks and the commissary. As she fell, she screamed at him one last time, calling him a murderer. Doyle admitted his guilt but deserted before going to trial.

In a literal instance of dirty laundry, two soldiers' wives at Fort Keogh, Montana, got into an argument in the 1890s because one had burned her trash too close to the other's hanging laundry. One woman threatened the other with a baseball bat. An unfortunate private, armed with an outdated bayonet and rifle, was assigned the task of walking back and forth between their quarters to keep the peace. This caused the women to forget their disagreement, and they instead took out their anger on the private.

⋖◈⋗

Fighting was not the only transgression of laundresses. Prostitution was a fact of life at many of the military posts. The military officially frowned upon this, but accepted it in a "don't ask, don't tell" manner. Sometimes, laundresses augmented their pay by working as prostitutes, and the term "laundress" became a euphemism for prostitute in some company.

Because prostitution was common at the military outposts, so were sexually transmitted diseases. At Fort Buford, North Dakota, on July 4, 1868, ten men reported to sick call; seven had some type of venereal disease.

In 1816, orders stated that no woman infected with venereal disease would be allowed to remain with the army or draw rations. One might question how this order was enforced, especially on the frontier where the women had virtually nowhere else to go. At Fort Davis, Texas, a number of laundresses and hospital matrons were fired and repeatedly rehired over a period of one year. This may have been an example of the post surgeon trying to comply with the 1816 regulations.

The sutler's store or post trader's store sometimes doubled as a base for prostitution. In 1866, an officer killed an enlisted man at a sutler's store. This resulted in an order that all women must leave the post unless they were authorized laundresses. If one reads between the lines, the men's disagreement must have involved a woman who was a pseudo-laundress, someone not officially sanctioned to be a laundress on the post.

At Fort Selden, New Mexico, in 1868, the post trader and the commander got into an argument, and several civilian men were kicked off the post. These men, including a whiskey dealer and a stage driver, went to the district commander, claiming that the post commander allowed prostitutes to live at the post trader's store. Captain J. G. Tilford responded, saying women did live at the store but he believed they were employed as servants. He acknowledged that one of the women was a laundress and did live at the store with a soldier, but he was unsure whether the woman and the soldier were married. He concluded his response by questioning whether prostitution at the fort should be the business of whiskey dealers and stage drivers. No reply ever appeared from the superior officers.

Other camp followers also provided sexual services for the troops and may have done so under the guise of "laundresses." At one point, letters sent to company commanders of the Sixth Infantry

Companies A, G, and I, and the Sixth Cavalry, Troop F, required commanders to furnish the names of their authorized laundresses, confirming whether or not they actually did laundry for the men. One can guess what suspicions led to a requirement to confirm that a laundress did laundry.

The legends surrounding Calamity Jane sometimes report her working for the military as a laundress, teamster, nurse, and scout, but there is no record of her being employed by the military in any of those capacities. She was a camp follower who did occasionally drive a wagon and nurse soldiers. She may have washed clothes or done some scouting, sometimes dressed as a man, while working for a civilian contractor or as a volunteer. However, General George Cook reportedly said he had no contact with her at all "except to order her out of camp when he discovered her . . . "

A Fort Brown, Texas, laundress may have engaged in prostitution. Records do not name her, nor do they reflect any deeper reason that Private John H. Williams, Ninth Cavalry, G Troop, left the troops' horses to graze unguarded for approximately one hour. However, he was visiting the laundress during this time. At his court-martial, he was found guilty of leaving his duties. He did hard labor for four months and was fined four month's pay as punishment. It would seem harsh punishment if he had been discussing dirty clothing with the laundress. It is unknown if the laundress faced any consequences.

Enlisted men were not the only ones who managed to run afoul of regulations with laundresses. An unpopular, foul-mouthed captain with the Seventh Cavalry was brought up on charges for immoral behavior. Among the charges was that he was drinking with a laundress as they rode in an ambulance on a march. Later he was seen in her tent. Additionally, he had a soldier drive him and two laundresses to a nearby hostelry where the debauchery continued. All this was done with the full knowledge of the enlisted men. The officer was court-martialed and relieved of his command, with half pay for a year.

At Fort Union, New Mexico, in January 1877, Mrs. Maria Straw, married to Ninth Cavalry Band member Patrick Straw, was quarantined with chancroid, a sexually transmitted bacterial infection. The post surgeon claimed he quarantined her to prevent contagion among the troops. One cannot assume this was the result of an extramarital affair on the part of Patrick. Obviously, Mrs. Straw was suspected of engaging in sexual activities with other men or she would not have been quarantined. It is unknown if this enhanced the family finances, but it would not have been uncommon for Patrick to have known about and encouraged his wife's entrepreneurship. The post surgeon's entry in the log gave no indication that this was unusual behavior. Army Surgeon D. C. Peters did note that had Mrs. Straw not been quarantined, she could have bathed in a hot springs about five miles from the post. Medical personnel at the time believed that "taking the baths" relieved "chronic, syphilitic complaints."

Laundresses, even the many who lived respectable lifestyles, may have been responsible for the spread of other diseases, as well. A smallpox epidemic raced through Fort Union, New Mexico, in 1877. Post Surgeon Dr. Cavallo did his best to control the epidemic, to no avail. The doctor believed that the source of the disease was a woman named Sylvia Francisco. She worked as a servant and had been a laundress. Cavallo knew that Francisco traveled back and forth to the nearby notorious community of Loma Parda. This place was off-limits to soldiers, as it was well known for its brothels. There is no evidence that Francisco was a prostitute, but she may have carried the smallpox virus into the fort.

Mrs. Thomas Boch's story fits the stereotype of the "laundress as a prostitute" perfectly. Boch was a laundress for Ninth Infantry, Company A, at Fort McPherson, Nebraska, in the late 1870s. Private Patrick Moriarty, also of the Ninth Infantry, was charged with the rape and assault of Mrs. Boch. As is often the case, particularly then, Boch's unsavory reputation came out during the trial. Witnesses for both sides stated that Mrs. Boch was often in the company of

Although this photograph is often identified as Cathy Williams, the MLK Center, identifies it as Cathy's mother Martha Williams. The MLK Center was originally the Lincoln Colored Home and Orphanage in Pueblo, Colorado, where Martha Williams worked as a matron.

drunken enlisted men. The prosecution blamed her husband, who reportedly regularly invited soldiers to his home as drinking buddies. Moriarty claimed he was not the only soldier to have had sex with Mrs. Boch. But unfortunately, he was the one that Boch's sister caught in the act. Defense witnesses claimed they had seen not only Moriarty, but other men as well, hugging Mrs. Boch when drinking at the Boch home. Witnesses also testified they had seen Mrs. Boch in the company of prostitutes in North Platte, Nebraska. Furthermore, Mrs. Boch's own husband referred to her as a whore. At the end of the trial, Moriarity was convicted of unlawful entry and assault. He was not convicted of "intent to commit rape."

⟨⟩

Laundresses could be quite opinionated. Fort Stockton, Texas, was host to a dusty caravan that had the misfortune to arrive on a Sunday. The women in the caravan wanted their laundry done, but the laundresses refused because they did not work on Sundays. One lady in the party of travelers stated that their refusal spoke well of the laundresses' religious beliefs, but she felt the laundresses just had better things to do than washing on a Sunday.

Another laundress at Camp Halleck, Nevada, refused to do the laundry of a "gentle, Eastern girl," probably an officer's wife. Alas, the young woman had to do the laundry herself, reddening her knuckles.

Refusing to do laundry was one thing; overdoing it was another. The wife of Post Surgeon Charles Winne, at Fort Sidney, Nebraska, had some of her laundry ruined during washing. Her "wretched laundress" had used too much lye in the laundry, and Mrs. Winne's new nightgown was among the casualties.

A laundress at Fort Concho, Texas refused to leave the area of the post hospital after being fired for theft, lying, and general impudence. She was persuaded to leave by a group of soldiers. A short two weeks later, three more laundresses were fired, this time by Captain Nicholas Nolan, for being "utterly worthless, drunk, and lewd."

Former slave Cathy Williams saw service as both a laundress and a soldier. When she became free in 1861, she took a job as a cook with the Thirteenth Army Corps. Unfortunately, she did not know how to cook, so she was dismissed from that job. She was then hired as a laundress for the officers of the Eighth Indiana. She followed the unit on their Civil War campaigns and saw many fellow slaves gain their freedom. Eventually the Eighth Indiana settled into an encampment near Saint Louis, where many of the troops fell ill with dysentery. Cathy never became ill.

Next the regiment was dispatched to Pea Ridge, Arkansas. Her duties there included nursing the injured and the ill, as well as doing the laundry. Cathy was introduced to some of the Civil War's

ARMY OF THE UNITED STATES.

CERTIFICATE

OF DISABILITY   FOR DISCHARGE

William Cathey, a *private* of Captain *Clarkes*
Company, (*a.*) of the *Thirty Eighth* Regiment of the United States
Infantry was enlisted by *Maj. Merriam* of
the *38th* Regiment of *Infantry* at *Saint Louis Mo.*
on the *15th* day of *November*, 1866, to serve 3 years; he was born
in *Independence* in the State of *Missouri*, is *24*
years of age, *5* feet *9* inches high, *Black* complexion, *Black* eyes,
Black hair, and by occupation when enlisted a *Cook*. During the last two
months said soldier has been unfit for duty *60* days.* *This soldier has been under my*
command since May 20th 1867. At that time he was doing Laundry
duty at Fort Harker, Kansas. He was then and has been since, feeble both
physically, and mentally, and much of the time quite unfit for duty. The
origin of this infirmities is unknown to me.

STATION *Fort Bayard, N. M.*
DATE: *August 14, 1868*

                Charles E. Clarke
                Capt 38th Inf. Bvt Maj. USA
                        Commanding Company.

     I CERTIFY, that I have carefully examined the said *William Cathey Priv't*
of Captain *Charles E. Clarke (A.)* Company, and find him incapable of performing the duties of a
soldier because of† *a scrofulous and feeble habits. He is continually*
on sick report without benefit. He is unable to do military
duty and is unfit for any service involving the least expo-
sure. This condition dates prior to enlistment.
Disability 1/2

                D. L. Huntington
                Bt. Lt. Col. U.S.A. Surgeon, U.S.A.

DISCHARGED, this *Fourteenth* day of *October* 1868, at
Fort Bayard, N.M.

                Bt 38 Inf't
                      Commanding the Reg't. *First*

The Soldier desires to be addressed at
    Town *Alton* county *Madison* state *Illinois*

See Note 1 on the back of this.   †See Note 2 on the back of this

[A. G. O., No. 100 & 101—First.]   [DUPLICATE.]

---

*William Cathay's discharge papers say, in the upper block, that he is
"feeble both physically and mentally." In the lower block it states he is
incapable of performing his duties because of "a scrofulous and feeble
habit." He "is unable to do military duty and is unfit for any service."*
(National Archives)

first Buffalo Soldiers, the black soldiers serving in the western frontier. Her duties fluctuated from nurse to laundress, and by then she was even allowed to cook again, having picked up some cooking skills along the way.

The Eighth Indiana became part of General Philip Sheridan's command. On October 19, 1864, Confederate soldiers attacked their camp in what became known as the Battle of Cedar Creek, Virginia. Cathy and the other laundresses and camp followers fled, fearing for their lives.

The unit regrouped in Baltimore, Maryland. From there, they were sent to Georgia. The Eighth Indiana was mustered out of service in August 1865. Cathy loved army life and left with great sadness. The soldiers, in an act of kindness, purchased a ticket for Cathy to return home. She went from Virginia to Iowa and eventually wound up at Jefferson Barracks, Missouri.

Cathy wasn't happy with civilian life. In 1866, Cathy decided to disguise herself as a man and became William Cathay, so that she could join the army. Since she was tall for the time, at five-feet nine-inches, the ruse was easier to pull off. She served all over the western United States, including Kansas, Colorado, New Mexico, and the Southwest. Eventually, she became ill and a post physician discovered her cross-identity. She was discharged in October 1868 as unfit for duty and became a civilian again.

⋘⊰❀⊱⋙

Sometimes laundresses were involved in practical jokes. A doctor at Fort Jupiter, Florida, took life very seriously and was unable to understand when someone was joking. As a prank, some soldiers brought him up on charges of "trifling with the affections of a laundress." The laundress referred to had quite a reputation. The doctor, not understanding that this was a practical joke, mounted a defense. He wrote out a long statement and called numerous witnesses to attest to his good character and to confirm the questionable reputation of the laundress. He eventually understood that it was all a joke, but his reaction to that was not recorded.

Laundresses did not always stand safely on the sidelines during skirmishes and battle campaigns. Captain Pfeiffer, the commander at Fort Rae, New Mexico, suffered from rheumatism. Pfeiffer decided to partake of the soothing waters of a hot springs located about eight miles from the fort. He took a guard of six men, his wife, an Indian girl, and a laundress to keep him company as he soaked at Ojo Caliente. They took care in selecting a safe place to camp at the hot springs; however, they did not realize Apaches had followed them. That afternoon, the three women went for a walk while the captain soaked. The Apaches quickly captured the women and then used them as human shields in an attack on the camp. Two of the guards were immediately shot and killed. The captain, who was naked, jumped from the springs and ran to get his rifle from his tent. He took an arrow in the side, but managed to get across the river where he engaged in hand-to-hand combat with one of the Apaches, eventually killing the attacker. The rest of the Indians meanwhile raided the camp and fled, taking the three women with them as hostages. When word reached Fort Rae, soldiers rode in pursuit of the Apaches. The soldiers found two of the hostages dead at different locations along the way. The unnamed laundress was among the survivors and was able to tell the soldiers of her ordeal.

Even though some laundresses had hot tempers or questionable values, they served an important role in army life. Sometimes they were placed in danger; sometimes they placed others in danger. And yes, just like in society as a whole, some were more virtuous than others.

7. DIRTY LAUNDRY: *Biographical Notes*

Resources for this chapter include: *Glittering Misery: Dependents of the Indian Fighting Army* by Patricia Y. Stallard; *Daughters of Joy, Sisters of Misery: Prostitutes in the American West, 1865-90* by Anne M. Butler; *Army Wives on the American Frontier, Living by the Bugles* by Anne Burner Eales; *My Life in the Old Army: Reminiscences of Abner Doubleday; She Wore a Yellow Ribbon: Women Soldiers and Patriots of the Western Frontier* by JoAnn Chartier and Chris Enss; *Forty Miles a Day on Beans and Hay* by Don Rickey; *Memories of Long Ago* by Otto Louis Hein; *Class and Race in the Frontier Army: Military Life in the West, 1870-1890* by Kevin Adams; *Cathy Williams: From Slave to Female Buffalo Soldier* by Philip Thomas Tucker; *Army Sacrifices: Briefs from Official Pigeon-holes* by James Barnet Fry; *Trailing Clouds of Glory: Zachary Taylor's Mexican War Campaign and His Emerging Civil War Leaders* by Felice Flanery Lewis; *Men of Color to Arms! Black Soldiers, Indian Wars, and the Quest for Equality* by Elizabeth Leonard; and *Life of a Soldier on the Western Frontier* by Jeremy Agnew.

James D. McLaird's book *Calamity Jane: The Woman and the Legend* helped clarify the mythology surrounding Calamity Jane's supposed connection to the military.

I also referred to magazine and journal articles: "Army Laundresses: Ladies of the 'Soap Suds Row'" by Miller J. Stewart; "Laundresses: The Forgotten Women of the Frontier" by S. Hansen; and "Fort Union and the Frontier Army in the Southwest: A Historic Resource Study Fort Union National Monument Fort Union, New Mexico" by Leo E. Oliva. The *Bismarck Tribune* has covered the story of Mrs. Nash in great detail both at the time of her death and periodically through the years.

I conducted on-site research at Fort Laramie, Wyoming, and Fort Totten, North Dakota.

9. Out with the Wash Water

SARAH OSBORN, Suzie King, Mrs. Nash, Ellen Williams, the Great Northern, and most of the other hardworking military laundresses were an asset to the army and provided a much needed service. But in 1876, the army became the focus of reorganization hearings in Congress. Laundresses became a major concern in the hearings. The House Committee on Military Affairs (the Banning Committee) investigated the subject. Members of the committee found the military held two different viewpoints concerning whether laundresses should be retained by the army.

General George Sykes presented arguments both for and against their retention. He said that by doing away with the laundress position "a great drag would be removed from the service." Laundresses cost the military budget not only monetarily, but also in time and effort to move and manage them on a post. Expense was one of the major arguments for eliminating the position.

General John C. Kelton felt that discharging the estimated 1,720 laundresses would be financially beneficial, saving approximately $154,800 per year in rations alone. He estimated that one-tenth of transportation costs would be saved and one-twentieth of building and quarters repair budget could be cut by either having soldiers or civilians do the laundry. Captain Henry Thomas also considered economic factors. He figured the army could save six percent on the cost of rations and seventeen percent on transportation.

Inspector General Randolph B. Marcy had his set of figures, too. He said the army was authorized to have 1,316 laundresses (the figure differs from Kelton's.) He believed the laundresses were paid well for their work, and they also drew rations worth $100,000 per year. He concluded that it cost $200,000 a year to move the laundresses as they had so much baggage and equipment and many had children. Fuel to heat their quarters was another expense. He acknowledged that much of the housing was substandard, despite the additional expense.

Colonel R. I. Dodge wanted the laundresses gone. He indirectly brought up the prostitution angle by saying, "It is an absurd continuation of a custom which grew out of other wants of the men in the company than washing clothes."

Captain Henry G. Thomas also believed the institution of laundresses needed to end. His objections included the fact that if a laundress's child became ill, her soldier husband had to take time off from his job to care for the child so the laundress could continue her work. He said it was unfair that some soldiers—those married to laundresses—had more money and were allowed the comforts of being married while others did not. Thomas did not believe the laundresses had a refining effect on the soldiers and felt photographs of laundresses proved that fact.

Among the advocates for keeping laundresses, General Sykes, who had already pointed to their expense, straddled the fence and argued that laundresses were beneficial, especially at the remote posts. He thought they were a positive influence on the soldiers and stated that the soldiers liked to talk to the laundresses, and they made the men more content.

General Kelton also saw both advantages and disadvantages. He echoed Sykes's feelings in some regards. While agreeing that it would save money to dispose of laundresses, he thought it would be detrimental. Kelton stated, "Laundresses are necessary to garrison life for their far greater purposes than as washerwomen, and their children are as neat and as charming as may be found in any community." Kelton also indicated that removing the laundresses might bring "immorality, dishonor, and dishonesty" to the forts. He felt

A laundress who started out as a single woman often married and her family grew. She was still allowed to stay with her regiment even as her family expanded, but moving large families with the troops became a more complicated and expensive process. (Library of Congress)

this would make it necessary for other women and children to leave the garrison for their own safety.

General Edward O. C. Ord thought laundresses made the men happier and kept them honest and that married men made the best soldiers. He testified that laundresses were honest, married women, and he feared that discharging laundresses would cause their husbands to resign, due to the low wages the army paid the soldiers. He also noted that the enlisted men liked the homey atmosphere on Suds Row. Ord even recommended that the number of laundresses in the companies made up of black men be doubled, so the men would not miss the company of women.

Colonel Samuel D. Sturgis and Brigadier General Christopher C. Auger agreed that the laundresses should be kept on, as they were necessary. Both men had spent many years on the western frontier and were familiar with the laundresses and the roles they played at the more remote military outposts.

Several officers worried about the laundresses losing their jobs. Captain Thomas did not want their jobs to end immediately, nor did he think they should have to quit at the end of their husband's enlistment. Inspector General Marcy recommended that no more married men be allowed to enlist in the army. He suggested that the army look carefully at any currently enlisted men who were married to laundresses. Under his plan, when their hitch was done, they would not be allowed to reenlist unless special circumstances called for it.

On June 19, 1876, new orders were issued. General Order 37 stated: "Hereafter, women shall not be allowed to accompany troops as laundresses." The order did not prohibit the women from staying with their companies until their husbands fulfilled their enlistments. Laundress benefits were determined individually. As late as 1880, a Fort Totten laundress was authorized by Special Orders No. 122 to travel via government transportation to join her soldier husband's company.

Laundresses also continued to receive rations, but this changed on April 10, 1883, when Army Circular No. 3 came out, stating that laundresses would no longer receive rations after June 18. As late as 1893, quarters were still provided for laundresses at Fort Buford, North Dakota. The Fort Meade, South Dakota, Post Order Book 117 contained a circular pertaining to laundresses. It directed the company commanders to inspect the laundresses and other soldiers' family quarters.

For eighty years, the army provided a much-needed service to the troops and provided many women with jobs when few were available. The women added to the atmosphere at the military posts, mostly in a positive manner. They were among the first women to reside in some isolated parts of the frontier and saw this country taking shape. An essential part of military life, they are, however, the forgotten members of the military.

Henceforth from 1876, enlisted men or civilians would wash a soldier's laundry. In 1892, Civil War nurses were made eligible for pensions, but not laundresses.

9. OUT WITH THE WASH WATER: *Bibliographical Notes*

The main resources for this chapter include: *Glittering Misery: Dependents of the Indian Fighting Army* by Patricia Y. Stallard, and "Army Laundresses: Ladies of the 'Soap Suds Row'" by Miller J. Stewart.

I conducted personal research at Fort Buford, North Dakota.

Appendix
Registry of Known Laundresses

This is a registry of known laundresses and facts about their lives. It is by no means complete. Throughout this list where geographical information is designated, current states are used to provide a better frame of reference. At the time the laundresses were stationed at the various posts, the forts may have actually been located in a territory.

Readers are welcomed and encouraged to send additions to the list. Names and documentation should be sent through my email address listed on my website <www.armylaundress.com>.

Anghey, Elizabeth. Born in 1842, in Canada. Married, Thomas Angey (note different spelling). Fort Laramie, 1870.

Andrews, (Unknown). Married. Fort Hays, KS, 1874. Assigned to House Number 2 on Laundress Row.

Anthony, (Unknown). Fort Laramie, 1878. 3rd Cavalry, Co. B.

Augusheimer, Mrs. Fort Laramie, 1878. 3rd Cavalry, Co. A.

Baker, Jane. Born in Prussia, 1825. Fort Laramie, 1860. 10th Infantry, Co. C.

Baxter, (Unknown). Possibly Mrs. Charles A. Baxter. Fort Laramie, 1872.

Bergsland, Regina. Fort Hays, KS, 1874. Assigned to House Number 13 on Laundress Row. Was relieved as a matron in the post hospital in 1876.

Berthram, (Unknown). Married to Pvt. Charles Berthram. Fort Hays, KS, 1872. 6th Cavalry.

Boch, Mrs. Thomas. Married. Fort McPherson, NE, late 1870s. 9th Infantry, Co. A.

Boerner, (Unknown). Married to Comm. Sgt. Ernest Boerner. Fort Hays, KS, 1874. 23rd Infantry. A daughter was born at Fort Hays, August 11, 1878.

Bolan, (Unknown). Fort Hays, KS, 1871. Was the wife of a tent maker (name unknown) employed by the QMD. Occupied House Number One on Laundress Row.

Botzer, (Unknown). Married to Edward Botzer who was born in Germany in 1845. Fort Hays, KS. 7th Cavalry, Troop G. This laundress had special orders on April 26, 1869 to join her company at Fort Hays. Mother's name was Brush. Brother named Charlie. Edward Botzer was discharged as a Corporal in 1871 and reenlisted. He was a First Sergeant with the 7th Cavalry, Co. G in 1876 when he was killed crossing the Little Big Horn River. His remains were found in 1989 in the bank of the Little Big Horn River at the site of Reno's retreat crossing.

Bourgette, Sarah. Married several husbands. 1840s, 7th Infantry. Was also know by several other names including Sarah Bowman, Borginnis, Davis, and Knight, as well as the Great Northern, the Great Western, and the Heroine of Fort Brown.

Brewster, (Unknown). Married to Pvt. George W. Brewster. Fort Bridger, 1868. 36th Infantry, Co. H.

Brown, Rachel Lobach. Married, Sgt. Henry Brown. Ft. Bridger, WY, 1987. Likely a laundress.

Brownell, Kady. Born 1842 in South Africa. Married to Robert Brownell. 1st and 5th Rhode Island. Present at First Bull Run and the Battle of New Berne, North Carolina. Was a *vivandière*. May have actually worked as a laundress. Was a color (flag) carrier for her unit. She received an army pension of $8.00 per month, beginning in 1884.

Brush, (Unknown). Married. Fort Hays, KS. 7th Cavalry, Troop G. This laundress had special orders on April 26, 1869, to join her company at Fort Hays. This may have been either Mrs. Botzer, or her mother.

Burton, Martha. Fort Hays, KS, March 20, 1869 to March 28, 1869. 10th Cavalry, Troop B. She was sent to Fort Dodge from Fort Riley, via Fort Hays. She was to proceed to Fort Dodge to join her company.

Cavanaugh, Mrs. Married. Camp McDermitt, NV.

Cloonan, Bridget. Born in Ireland, maiden name Malloy. Married to Sgt. Patrick Cloonan, August 3, 1873, Fort Union, New Mexico. 8th US Cavalry, Company B. Departed Fort Union in 1876.

Cornwall, (Unknown). Married to David Cornwall. Continental Army, September 1780.

Coyle, Ellen. Born in Ireland. Married to Joseph. Fort Laramie, 1880-1883. Children in 1880 included: Mary, 12; Agnes, 11; and William, 7.

Crisp, Sarah. Born in 1832 in New York. Fort Laramie, 1860. 10th Infantry, Co. C.

Cromine, Matilda. Born 1835 in Ireland. Fort Laramie, 1870. 4th Infantry.

Curnan, Mrs. Annie. Fort Wallace, KS, 1868. Co. I.

Dabney, Mrs. Civil War, Union Forces, 1863. Passed Confederate information to her husband on the Union side.

Davis, Julia. Born 1840, in Ireland. Fort Laramie, 1870. 4th Infantry. One known child, a girl born October 19,1868.

Delapp, Emma. Fort Buford, ND, 1872. Died September 9, 1872 at Fort Buford of phthisis (tuberculosis).

Deaver, Bridget. 1864. 1st Michigan Cavalry, Civil War and later with a regiment of the regular army on the plains. Also known as Irish Biddy, and Michigan Bridget. She was known to take the place of fallen soldiers during battle.

Deyan, Ann. Born 1851 in Ireland. Fort Laramie, 1870. 4th Infantry.

Dolan, Bridget. Born 1845 in Ireland. Fort Laramie, 1870. 4th Infantry.

Dolan, (Unknown). Fort Hays, KS, 1869. Dolan (rank unknown) and his wife were ordered off of the military reservation. They were occupying rooms in the laundress quarters. If they did not comply and move, they were to be forcibly ejected.

Douglas, (Unknown). Fort Bridger, WY, 1868. 36th Infantry, Co. B.

Duncan, (Unknown). Fort Laramie, 1872. Post Adjt. Wm. W. McCammon ordered repairs to her quarters, necessary to render them as comfortable as possible, December 1, 1872.

Dunlap, Mary. Born 1848 in Michigan. Fort Laramie, 1868–1870. 4th Infantry.

Durand, Emma. Fort Buford, ND, 1881. Died February 14, 1881, at Fort Buford. Was reburied at Custer National Cemetery, Section A, Grave Number 395.

Dwier, I. Fort Hays, KS, 1871. Married. 6th Infantry, Co. A. Occupied House Number 2.

Early, Bridget. Born 1835 in Ireland. Fort Laramie, 1868. 4th Infantry. One known child, born November 14, 1868.

Egan, (Unknown). Fort Laramie, 1872. 4th Infantry. On May 23, 1872 she was ordered to leave the post because of scandalous and disrespectful conduct. (General Order #24)

Eichler, Margaret. Born in Pensylvania. Married to Pvt. Robert Eichler, born in Germany. Fort Hays, KS, 1880. Age 25 in 1880. 4th Cavalry Band. Daughter Minn, 7 in 1880, was born in Missouri; daughter Maria, 4 in 1880, was born in Indian Territory; and daughter Emilia, 1 in 1880, was born in Texas.

Eldridge, Mrs. Fort Hays, KS, May 1874. Assigned to House Number 5 on Laundress Row.

Elkhorn, Mary. Born 1832 in Ireland. Fort Laramie, 1860. 10th Infantry, Co. D.

Fircetta, (Unknown). Fort Hays, KS, November 1871. Married. Occupied House Number 3 on Laundress Row.

Fitsgerald, (Black) Susan. Fort Phil Kearny, WY, 1867. 18th Infantry. Company H.

Fitzgerald, Annie. Fort Laramie, 1878. 3rd Cavalry, Co. A.

Fitzgerald, Mary A., Mrs. Fort Hays, KS, May 1870. Married to Ord. Sgt. Michael Fitzgerald. 7th Cavalry, Troop G. She was to be provided with a monthly certificate for her rations. On May 20, 1870, she was provided with her laundress certificate for the above assignment. On August 1, 1870, a certificate was required by the company commander in order for her to continue to draw rations. On August 3, she was no longer a laundress for 7th Cavalry, Troop G. On August 5, she was reappointed to her duties. In November 1871, she was listed as a laundress for the 6th Cavalry, Troop F. She and her husband occupied House Number 3 on Laundress Row. On January 1, 1874, she was reassigned as a hospital matron. In May of that year, she was assigned to House Number 12 on Laundress Row. In September, she was relieved of her duties as a hospital matron.On March 1, 1875, on the recommendation of the surgeon, A. K. Smith, a Mrs. Susan Torreus was relieved of her duties as a hospital matron, and Mrs. Fitzgerald was appointed instead. In June 1876, she was again appointed as a hospital matron.

Flood, Maggie. Married to Corporal Patrick Flood. Fort D.A. Russell, WY, 1875; Fort Laramie, 1877–79; Fort McKinney, WY, 1880. 3rd Cavalry, Co. A. Children: John, William, and Charles. Died December 7, 1929, in San Diego.

Fossette, (Unknown). Fort Hays, KS. Married to Sgt. Fossette, 6th Infantry.

Francisco, Sylvia. Fort Union, NM, 1877.

Franks, (Unknown). Was somehow associated with the 7th Cavalry, Troop F. Special Orders #44, dated April 26, 1869, state that Mrs. Franks is to join the company at Fort Hays.

French, (Unknown). Married to Serrin J. French. Possibly Fort Laramie, WY.

Funk, Laura. Married to Trumpeter Adam Funk. Fort Hays, KS, 1871–1874. 6th Cavalry, Troop F. Occupied House Number 4 on Laundress Row.

Geer, (Unknown). Married to George Geer, a civilian Fort Laramie, 1880. 3rd Cavalry, Co. L. One known child, a girl born April 1, 1880.

Gill, Julia. Married to Leodegar Schnyder, 1864. Fort Laramie, Civil War, 11th Ohio. Came to Fort Laramie with her sister Margaret Litsinger, also a laundress. Gill's nickname was "Cross-eyed Julia."

Glynn, Margaret. Born 1840 in Ireland. Fort Laramie, 1870. 4th Infantry.

Goodson, (Unknown). Married to Anson A. Goodson. Was no longer a laundress after June 30, 1878. 4th Infantry, Co. D.

Gratz, Kate. Fort Dodge, KS. 10th Cavalry, Troop K.

Hagen, Anna. Born 1830, Ireland. Fort Laramie, 1860. 2nd Dragoons, Co. F.

Hazen, May. Fort Buford, ND, 1872. Died July 4, 1872 at Fort Buford, of cholera.

Henry, Mrs. C. M. Fort Laramie, 1878. 3rd Cavalry, Co. A.

Hesler, Amy. Born 1838 in Ireland. Fort Laramie, 1870. 4th Infantry, Co. F.

Hess, Emeline Bigler. Born August 20, 1824, in Harrison County, Virginia. Married John W. Hess, Co. E, Mormon Battalion, 1846.

Hinsdale, Jane. 2nd Michigan Infantry, Co. D, Civil War.

Holbrook, (Unknown). Married to Calvin B. Holbrook. Was also listed as Mrs. Holebrock. Fort Laramie, 1864. 11th Ohio, Co. G.

Hurley, (Unknown). The post Adjt. Wm. M. McCammon ordered repairs to her quarters necessary to render them as comfortable as possible on December 1, 1872. Fort Laramie.

Johnson, Kate. Born in 1841 in Prussia. Fort Laramie, 1870. 4th Infantry.

Henry, Lizzie. Fort Laramie, 1877. 3rd Cavalry, Co. F.

Hurlbut, (Unknown). Fort Lapwai, ID, 1877. Married, her husband was killed in a battle with the Nez Perce. She had an unknown number of children. Her husband died before the birth of one of the children.

Kapp, Margaret. Born 1850 in Ireland. Fort Laramie, 1870. 4th Infantry.

Kelly, Mrs. Ft. Harker, KS. Likely a laundress.

Kitchen, Anna. Born in Missouri. Married to George A. Kitchen. Fort Laramie, 1880. 5th Cavalry, Co. I. Father was born in Virginia; her mother was born in Kentucky. Her medical history includes the dates of May 21, 1880, and August 6, 1880. A child, Walter M. died August 6, 1880 at the age of 10 months and 2 days. The cause of death was listed as diarrhea. On December 17, 1880, a baby daughter was born.

Klawitter, Mrs. Fred. Wife of Fred, Fort Lincoln, ND, 1870s. Likely a laundress.

Knott, Elizabeth. Died February 27, 1871 at Fort Buford, ND, of disease.

Kreyser, (Unknown). Fort Laramie, 1877–1878. 3rd Cavalry, Co. F.

Ladendorf, Mary. Born 1825 in Ireland. Fort Laramie, 1860? 2nd Dragoons, Co. D.

Leahy, Mrs. Camp Date Creek, AZ.

Leonard, Margaret. Married to Newton Leonard. Second Massachusetts Heavy Artillery, Civil War.

Litsinger, Margaret. Fort Laramie, Civil War. Came to Fort Laramie during the Civil War with her sister Julia Gill.

Littlejohn, Margaret. Born 1842, the daughter of D. and M. M. Caton, Owen County, Missouri. Married to Amos W. Littlejohn. Fort Buford, ND, 1878. 6th Infantry, Co. I. Died October 5, 1878 at Fort Buford, ND. Original grave at Fort Buford, reburied in Custer National Cemetery, Grave A–136.

Loynes, Mrs. Fort Keogh, MT, 1877-78. Troop E.

Lucinda (no last name given). Civil War, 1864. 13th Connecticut Volunteers. Company A. She was a black laundress.

Mahedy, (Unknown). Married to James Mahedy. Fort Laramie, 1878. 4th Infantry, Co. D. Was no longer a laundress after June 1878.

Mahoney, (Unknown). Fort Laramie, 1860. 9th Infantry, Co. E.

Maroney, Bridget. Born 1834. Fort Laramie, 1860, 10th Infantry, Co. C.

McGowen, (Unknown). Married to soldier McGowen, rank unknown. Fort Point, California, 1861. 9th Infantry, Co. F.

Montgomery, (Unknown). Married to Private John M. Montgomery. Fort Union, NM. 15th Infantry, Co. C.

Morony, (Unknown). Married to Sergeant Patrick Marony (different spelling). Fort Leavenworth, KS, Fort Scott, UT, 1857. Personal laundress and cook for Lieutenant Jesse Grove. Son, Johnny. This woman was an excellent cook. She served canned tongue, biscuits, butter, salad, and more to the lieutenant. He cheerfully admitted she was "one of the best women in the army."

Morris, May. Fort Laramie, 1874. 14th Infantry, Co. K. Morris was a replacement for Mrs. Vanhorten. Morris had already drawn rations as a hospital matron at Fort Laramie.

Morry, Bridget. Born 1842 in Ireland. Fort Laramie, 1870. 4th Infantry.

Mooty, (Unknown). Fort Laramie, 1878. 3rd Cavalry, Co. K.

Murphy, (Unknown). Fort Laramie, 1878. Married to John D. Murphy. 3rd Cavalry, Co. F.

Nash, Mrs. Married to several soldiers including Clifford (Clifton), Nash, and Cloonan. Elizabethtown, KY, and Dakotas, 1866-1878. 7th Cavalry. Died October 29, 1878, Fort Abraham Lincoln, ND. Discovered at death to be transgendered.

O'Brien, Ann. Born in Ireland, 1842. Fort Laramie, 1870. 4th Infantry. Children were Ann F., Mary F., and Eliza J.

O'Brien, Annie. Born in Ireland, 1840. Married to John D. O'Brien. Fort Laramie, 1870. Children were John, William, and Mary. Twins James and Thomas were born March 15, 1869, at Fort Laramie. 4th Infantry.

Osborn(e), Sarah. Both laundress and cook, Continental Army.

Patten, (Unknown). Born in Ireland. Fort D. A. Russell, WY.

Ramis, (Unknown). Fort Union, NM. 8th Cavalry, Troop L.

Raney, Eliza. Born in England, 1825. Fort Laramie, 1860. 2nd Dragoons, Co. F.

Roach, Julia. Fort C. F. Smith, MT. Buried at Custer National Cemetery, Section B, #324.

Ross, (Unknown). Married to Charles G. Ross. Fort Laramie, 1878. 3rd Cavalry, Co. K.

Rooney, Rose Quinn. 15th Louisiana Regiment, Co. K, June 1861, throughout the Civil War.

Rozsa, Patience. Married to John. Fort Scott, UT.

Scully, (Unknown). Married to Sgt. Scully. Fort Laramie, 1877. 9th Infantry, Co. E.

Sears, Mary. Born in Ireland, 1834. Fort Laramie, 1870. 4th Infantry.

Selzengee, (Unknown). 11th Ohio, Co. E.

Smith, (first name unknown). Sitka, AK, 1874.

Smith, Agatha. Born in Bavaria, 1836. Fort Laramie, 1870. 4th Infantry.

Smith, Minnie. Fort Buford, ND, 1893. Died, September 9, 1893 at Fort Buford. Reburied at Custer National Cemetery, Plot Number 373.

Smith, Rosanna. Born in Holland, 1835. Fort Laramie, 1860. 10th Infantry, Co. K.

Stanley, Jane. Born in Norwegia, 1833. Fort Laramie, 1860. 10th Infantry, Co. K.

Stine (Steine), Ellen. Born in Ireland. Married to Daniel Stine in 1860. Fort Laramie, 1860. Child was Fredrick, born in 1861.

Straw, Maria. Married to Patrick Straw, 9th Cavalry Band. Fort Union, NM, 1877.

Stuart, Mary. Fort Stockton, TX, 1879. 10th Cavalry.

Sullivan, Alice. Born in Ireland, maiden name was Murphy. Married John, in Glin, West Limerick County, Ireland, 1875. Fort Bridger, 1878–1879. 4th Infantry, Co. I. Children were one girl and one boy, Daniel, born at Fort Bridger, and two more girls and one boy born at other military posts.

Sullivan, Mary. Married. 18th Volunteer Infantry. Mrs. Sullivan was issued a transportation pass on March 31, 1863, to travel on the steamer Champion from St. Louis to Memphis to rejoin her regiment.

Taylor, Susie King. Born August 6, 1878 into slavery. Civil War. 1862 became a laundress for the 1st South Carolina Volunteers (33rd USCT). Served as a laundress, cook, seamstress, and nurse.

Thompson, Annie Elizabeth. Married to Archie Thompson. Fort Laramie, 1878. Listed also as Annie Elizabeth George (maiden name?).

Trainor, (Unknown). Married to Sergeant Trainor. Fort Point, CA 1861. 9th Infantry, Co. F.

Tubman, Harriet. Well-known black humanitarian, and, during the Civil War, a Union spy. Born into slavery she escaped and helped many family members and others to freedom. Served as a cook, nurse, and laundress.

Vanhouten, (Unknown). Fort Laramie, 1872–1874. 4th Infantry, Co. K.

Volener, (Unknown). Fort Laramie, 1878. 3rd Cavalry, Co. K.

Weir, Mrs. 1811–1812.

White, Mary. Born 1832 in Norwegia. Fort Laramie, 1860. 10th Infantry, Co. K.

Williams, Cathy. Freed slave, 1861. Laundress, cook, nurse, 8th Indiana. Civil War, 1861–1865. Aka: William Cathay.

Williams, Ellen. Born 1828 in England, maiden name Barber. Married to Charles Williams, United States, 1851. 2nd Colorado Cavalry, Co. A.

Wooster, (Unknown). Fort Laramie, 1872. Post Adjt. Wm. M. M. Mc-Cammon ordered repairs to her quarters, necessary to render them as comfortable as possible on December 1, 1872.

Young, Mrs. Continental Army, 1780. Widow of Peter Young.

BIBLIOGRAPHY

Adams, Kevin. *Class and Race in the Frontier Army: Military Life in the West, 1870-1890*. Norman, OK: University of Oklahoma Press, 2009.

Agnew, Jeremy. *Life of a Soldier on the Western Frontier*. Missoula, MT: Mountain Press Publishing, 2008.

The American Pageant. 7th ed. United States: D.C. Heath and Company, 1983.

"The Army Laundress." Accessed June 12, 2013. http://www.fortconcho. com/laundress.htm.

Army Regulations, Adopted for the Use of the Army of the Confederate States, in Accordance with Late Acts of Congress. Revised from the Army Regulations of the Old U.S. Army 1857; Retaining All That Is Essential for Officers of the Line. To Which Is Added an Act for the Establishment and Organization of the Army of the Confederate States of America. Also Articles of War, for the Government of the Army of the Confederate States of America. New Orleans: Bloomfield & Steel, 1861.

Barnett, Louise K. *Ungentlemanly Acts: The Army's Notorious Incest Trial*. New York: Hill and Wang, 2000.

"Before There Were Washboards…" Accessed June 18, 2015. www.oldandinteresting.com/washingbeetles-possing.aspx

Brown, Dee. *The Gentle Tamers*. New York: Bantam Books, 1958.

Brown, Orson P. (Family). "The Life, Times and Family of Orson Pratt Brown. John W. Hess." Accessed May 15, 2015. www.orsonpratt-brown.com/CJB/02Susan-Foutz/John-w-hess1824-1903html

—— "The Life, Times, and Family of Orson Pratt Brown. Women of the Mormon Battalion 1846-1848." www.orsonprattbrown.com/Mormon Battalion/women-children1847.mb/html

Bryk, N., ed. *American Dress Pattern Catalogs, 1873-1909.* Mineola, NY: Dover Publications, 1988.

Butler, Anne M. *Daughters of Joy, Sisters of Misery: Prostitutes in the American West, 1865-90.* Urbana: University of Illinois Press, 1985.

Cardoza, Thomas. *Intrepid Women: Cantinières and Vivandières of the French Army.* Bloomington: Indiana University Press, 2010.

Carrington, Frances C. *My Army Life and the Fort Phil Kearney Massacre.* Lincoln and London: University of Nebraska Press, 2004.

Carrington, Margaret. *Absaraka, Home of the Crows: A Military Wife's Journal Retelling Life on the Plains and Red Cloud's War.* New York: Skyhorse Publishing, 2015

Carvallo, Carlos. *Extract from Sanitary Report,* April 30, 1881, Section Two. Fort Laramie National Historic Site Laundress Guide, p. L-8

Chartier, JoAnn, and Chris Enss. *She Wore a Yellow Ribbon: Women Soldiers and Patriots of the Western Frontier.* Guilford, CT: TwoDot, 2004.

Chartrand, Rene. *Uniforms and Equipment of the United States Forces in the War of 1812.* Youngstown, NY: Old Fort Niagara Association, Inc., 1992.

Convis, Charles L. *True Tales of the Old West.* Carson City, NV: Pioneer Press, 2004.

Corbusier, Fanny Dunbar and Patricia Y. Stallard. *Fanny Dunbar Corbusier: Recollections of her Army Life, 1869-1908.* Norman: University of Oklahoma Press, 2003.

Cordell, Linda S., Kent Lightfoot, Francis McManamon, and George Milner. *Archaeology in America: An Encyclopedia.* Westport: Greenwood Publishing Group, 2008.

Courtwright, David T. *Violent Land: Single Men and Social Disorder from the Frontier to the Inner City*. Cambridge, MA: Harvard University Press, 1996.

Cox-Paul, Lori A., and James W. Wengert. *A Frontier Army Christmas*. Lincoln, Neb.: Nebraska State Historical Society, 1996.

Cozzens, Peter, Charles King, and Wesley Merritt. *Eyewitnesses to the Indian Wars, 1865-1890*. Mechanicsburg, PA: Stackpole Books, 2001.

Crotty, Rob. The National Archives, Prologue: "Pieces of History, Confederate Dirty Laundry: Spies and Slaves." Accessed October 12, 2015. http://blogs.archives.gov/prologue/?p=3852

Cunnington, C. Willett, and Phillis Cunnington. *The History of Underclothes*. New York: Dover Publishing, 1992.

Custer, Elizabeth Bacon. *Boots and Saddles; Or, Life in Dakota with General Custer*. Norman: University of Oklahoma Press, 1961.

Daniel, Larry J. *Soldiering in the Army of Tennessee: A Portrait of Life in a Confederate Army*. Chapel Hill: University of North Carolina Press, 1991.

Ditmore, Melissa H. *Encylopedia of Prostitution and Sex Work*. Vol. Two. Westport: Greenwood Publishing Group, 2006.

Doubleday, Abner, and Joseph E. Chance. *My Life in the Old Army: The Reminiscences of Abner Doubleday*. Ft. Worth: Texas Christian University Press, 1998.

Eales, Anne Bruner. *Army Wives on the American Frontier: Living by the Bugles*. Boulder, CO: Johnson Books, 1996.

Ferguson, Helen. "The Roles Women Played in the War of 1812." Accessed July 4, 2001. http://unbrigade.tripod.com/women.html

Field, Ron, and Adam Hook. *Forts of the American Frontier, 1820-91: The Southern Plains and Southwest*. Oxford: Osprey, 2006.

Fifer, Barbara, Fred Pflughoft, and David M. Morris. *Wyoming's Historic Forts*. Helena, MT: Farcountry Press, 2002.

FitzGerald, Emily McCorkle. *An Army Doctor's Wife on the Frontier: The Letters of Emily McCorkle FitzGerald from Alaska and the Far West 1874-1878*. Lincoln: University of Nebraska Press, 1962,

Foote, Cheryl J. *Women of the New Mexico Frontier, 1846-1912*. Niwot, CO: University Press of Colorado, 1990.

Frazer, Robert. *Forts of the West*. Norman: University of Oklahoma Press, 1972.

Fry, James B. *Army Sacrifices: Briefs from Official Pigeon-holes*. Mechanicsburg, PA: Stackpole Books, 2003.

Godfrey, Audrey M. "Housewives, Hussies, and Heroines, or the Women of Johnston's Army." *Utah Historical Quarterly*, Volume 54, Number 2, Spring 1986.

Gramm, Barbara Fairchild. *—and You Think You've Got It Bad: Turn-of-the-century Life & House-keeping*. St. Paul, MN: Pig's Eye Press, 1989.

Grassick, Mary K. *Fort Point: Fort Point National Historic Site, Presidio of California* 2, no. 2 (1994).

Graves, Dianne. *In the Midst of Alarms: The Untold Story of Women and the War of 1812*. Montreal, Canada: Robin Brass Studio, 2007.

Green, Carol Cranmer. *Chimborazo: The Confederacy's Largest Hospital*. Knoxville: University of Tennessee Press, 2007.

Greene, Jerome A. *Indian War Veterans: Memories of Army Life and Campaigns in the West, 1864-1898*. Havertown: Casemate Publishers, 2007.

Hansen, S. "The Forgotten Women of the Frontier." *History of the West*, December 10, 1985.

Henry, Robert S. *The Story of the Mexican War*. Boston: Da Capo Press, 1989.

Hess, J. W. "With the Mormon Battalion." *The Utah Historical Quarterly* 4 (April 1931).

Hein, Otto Louis. *Memories of Long Ago.* New York, G.P. Putman's Sons, 1925.

Hiley, M. *Victorian Working Women.* Boston: David Goodine, Publisher, 1979.

Hill, Thomas E. *The Essential Handbook of Victorian Etiquette.* San Francisco, CA: Bluewood Books, a Division of the Siyeh Group, 1994.

"History of Fort Schuyler." Accessed July 4, 2001. http://www.maritimeindustrymuseum.org/schuyler.html

Hoagland, A. K,. "Village Constructions: U.S. Army Forts on the Plains, 1848 - 1890." *Winterthur Portfolio* 34 (Winter 1999): 215-37.

Kimble, Jean H. "Susan Fitsgerald," in *Portraits of Fort Phil Kearny.* Banner, WY: The Fort Phil Kearny/Bozeman Trail Association, 1993.

Kimble, Jean H. And Susan Badger Doyle. "Tenador Ten Eyck," in *Portraits of Fort Phil Kearny.* Banner, WY: The Fort Phil Kearny/Bozeman Trail Association, 1993.

Larson, Kate Clifford. *Bound for the Promised Land: Harriet Tubman, Portrait of an American Hero.* New York: Ballantine, 2004.

Lavender, D. "Fort Laramie: Part 5 Life of the Soldier." *U.S. History,* September 1, 1990.

Laver, Harry S., and Jeffrey J. Matthews. *The Art of Command: Military Leadership from George Washington to Colin Powell.* Lexington, KY: University Press of Kentucky, 2008.

Leckie, William H., and Shirley A. Leckie. *The Buffalo Soldiers: A Narrative of the Black Cavalry in the West, Revised Edition.* Norman: University of Oklahoma Press, 2012.

Leonard, Elizabeth D. *Men of Color to Arms!: Black Soldiers, Indian Wars, and the Quest for Equality.* New York: W.W. Norton &, 2010.

Lewis, Felice Flanery. *Trailing Clouds of Glory: Zachary Taylor's Mexican War Campaign and His Emerging Civil War Leaders.* Tuscaloosa: University of Alabama Press, 2010.

Loynes, Charles N. "The Nez Perce War and the Battle of Big Hole, 1877," in *Indian War Veterans: Memories of Army Life and Campaigns in the West, 1864-1898.* New York and California: Savas Beatie, 2007.

Maghee, T. G., Dr. *Historical Blotter Notes for the Post History Camp Brown, Wyoming Territory.* 1876.

Markle, Donald E. *Spies and Spymasters of the Civil War.* New York: Hippocrene Books, 1994.

Mayer, Holly A. *Belonging to the Army: Camp Followers and Community during the American Revolution.* Columbia, SC: University of South Carolina Press, 1999.

McCaffrey, James M. *Army of Manifest Destiny: The American Soldier in the Mexican War, 1846-1848.* New York: New York University Press, 1992.

McKale, William, and William D. Young. *Fort Riley: Citadel of the Frontier West.* Topeka: Kansas State Historical Society, 2000.

McLaird, James D. *Calamity Jane: The Woman and the Legend.* Norman, Oklahoma: University of Oklahoma Press, 2005.

McManus, John C. *American Courage, American Carnage: 7th Infantry Chronicles: The 7th Infantry Regiment's Combat Experience, 1812 Through World War II.* New York: MacMillian, 2009.

McNeely, Regina Bennett. "Sarah Bowman." Handbook of Texas Online. Accessed October 15, 2015. http://www.tshaonline.org/handbook/online/articles/fbo30

Mescher, Virginia. "Tubs and Suds: Civil War Laundresses in the Field, Camp and Hospital. 2013.

Nacy, Michele. *Members of the Regiment: Army Officers' Wives on the Western Frontier, 1865-1890.* Westport, CT: Praeger, 2000.

Nix, D. K. "Common Law Marriage." Accessed July 20, 2013. http://www.donnix.com/common.htm

Oliva, Leo E. *Fort Dodge: Sentry of the Western Plains*. Topeka: Kansas State Historical Society, 1998.

———. *Fort Harker: Defending the Journey West*. Topeka: Kansas State Historical Society, 2000.

———. *Fort Hays: Keeping Peace on the Plains*. Topeka, KS: Kansas State Historical Society, 1996.

———. *Fort Scott: Courage and Conflict on the Border*. Topeka, KS: Kansas State Historical Society, 1996.

———. "Fort Union and the Frontier Army in the Southwest: A Historic Resource Study Fort Union National Monument Fort Union, New Mexico." 1993. Accessed July 19, 2013. http://www.nps.gov/history/historyonline_books/foun/chap4.html

Rickey, Don. *Forty Miles a Day on Beans and Hay; the Enlisted Soldier Fighting the Indian Wars*. Norman: University of Oklahoma Press, 2012.

Roberts, Annie Gibson. *A Summer on the Plains with Custer's 7th Cavalry: The 1870 Diary of Annie Gibson Roberts*. Edited by Brian C. Pohanka. Lynchburg, VA: Schroeder Publications, 2004.

Sambrook, Pamela. *Laundry Bygones*. Princes Risborough: Shire Publications, 1987.

Schroeder-Lein, Glenna R. *The Encyclopedia of Civil War Medicine*. Armonk, NY: M.E. Sharpe, 2008.

Seagraves, A. *Soiled Doves: Prostitution in the Old West*. Hayden, ID: Wesanne Publications, 1994.

Setnik, L. *Victorian Costume for Ladies 1860 to 1900*. Atglen, PA: Schiffer Publishing, 2000.

Smith, Shannon D. *Give Me Eight Men: Women and the Myth of the Fetterman Fight*. Lincoln & London: University of Nebraska Press, 2008.

Somak, Matt, "Dirty Laundry and Civil War Espionage" Mental Floss. Accessed October 12, 2015. http://mentalfloss.com/article/31812/dirty-laundry-and-civil-war-espionage

Stallard, Patricia Y. *Glittering Misery: Dependents of the Indian Fighting Army.* Norman: University of Oklahoma Press, 1978.

State Historical Society of North Dakota. "Unit 3: Set 6: Section 2: Army Food Improves ." Accessed February 13, 2015. history.nd.gov/textbook/unit3_comculon?unit3_6_2_intro.html

Stewart, Miller J. "Army Laundresses: Ladies of "Soap Suds Row"" *Nebraska History*, 1980th ser., 61, no. 4.

Summerhayes, Martha. *Vanished Arizona: Recollections of the Army Life of a New England Woman.* Lakeside Press, 1908.

Taylor, Susie King, and Patricia W. Romero. *A Black woman's Civil War Memoirs: Reminiscences of My Life in Camp with the 33rd U.S. Colored Troops, late 1st South Carolina Volunteers.* New York: M. Wiener Publishers, 1988.

Thomas, J. "Common Law Marriage." Accessed July 20, 2013. http://www.aaml.org/sites/default/files/MAT1o&_1.pdf.

Tobin, Debra. "From Suds to Strummin', Washboards are in Demand." 2010. Accessed June 12, 2015. http://www.antiquetrader.com/antiques/vintage_washboards_in_demand

Tucker, Phillip Thomas. *Cathy Williams: From Slave to Female Buffalo Soldier.* Mechanicsburg, PA: Stackpole Books, 2002.

Utley, Robert. "Fort Union National Monument: Part 2 The Civil War Era." *U. S. History*, September 1, 1990.

Utley, Robert M. *Cavalier in Buckskin: George Armstrong Custer and the Western Military Frontier.* Norman: University of Oklahoma Press, 2001.

Walkley, Christina, and Vanda Foster. *Crinolines and Crimping Irons: Victorian Clothes: How They Were Cleaned and Cared for.* London: Owen, 1978.

Ware, Eugene. *The Indian War of 1864.* Topeka, Kansas: Cane and Company. Accessed May 28, 2015. www.kancoll.org/books/ware/ew_ch12.htm

WebMD,LLL. Birth Control Timeline c. 2005-2015. Originally published July 17, 2003. Accessed December 20, 2015 www.medicinenet.com/script/main/art.asp?articlekey=52118

West, Elliott. *Growing up with the Country: Childhood on the Far Western Frontier.* Albuquerque: University of New Mexico Press, 1989.

Williams, Ellen. *Three Years and a Half in the Army* or *History of the Second Colorado.* New York: published for the author by Fowler and Wells, 1885.

White, C.B., Assistant Surgeon. White's medical report of 1868–1869 is referred to in a history written for the Dedication of the New York State Merchant Marine Academy, Fort Schuyler, New York City, May 21, 1938. The reference was found at http://www. maritimeindustrymuseum.org/schuyler.html and is titled "History of Fort Schuyler Maritime Industry Museum: History of Fort Schuyler.

Wilson, William Moss. "The Nashville Experiment" in the *New York Times,* December 5, 2013.

Yacovone, Donald. *Freedom's Journey: African American Voices of the Civil War.* Chicago: Lawrence Hill Books, 2004.

abortions, 77
adobe living quarters, 32, 68. *See also* housing
advertisements, *35*
African American laundresses. *See* black laundresses
alcohol, *52,* 88, 89–90
American Civil War, 45, 48–51, 64, 118
ammonia, 40
animal butchering, 33
Apache, 119
apartment housing, 68, 69, 70. *See also* housing
aprons, 78
army laundresses. *See* laundresses
"army pianos," 39
army soldiers. *See* soldiers
ash variation, 33, 37
assault and laundresses, 109–11, 114–15. *See also* murder
Auger, Christopher C., 124

bacon, 53, 54
Bacon, Mrs. Lydia B., 76
Baker, Jane, 23, 127
Baker, Susan. *See* Taylor, Susie King
Baldwin, Alice, 70, 91
bands, musical, 75, 88
barn housing, 63, 65. *See also* housing
baseball leagues, 88

bathing, 80–82
bats, laundry, 39
Battle of Cedar Creek, U.S. Civil War, 118
Battle of Yorktown, Revolutionary War, 17
beans, 53, 54
beef, 17, 48, 53, 54, 103
benefits for laundresses, 11, 17, 18, 51–61, 122. See also *specific benefits*
birth control, 76
Bismark Tribune, 108
Black, C. S., 68
black laundresses, *21,* 23, 47–48, 77, *115,* 116. *See also* laundresses
black soldiers, *21,* 23, 47, 118, 123. *See also* soldiers
Boch, Mrs. Thomas, 114, 128
boots, 78
Boots and Saddles (Custer), 110
Botzer, Mrs. Edward, 128
Bourgette, Sarah, 13, *99,* 100–102, *101,* 128
box irons, *43,* 44
Bragg, Braxton, 102
brothels, 64, 102, 114
Brown, Rachel Lobach, 104, 128
Brownell, Kady, *18,* 128
Buffalo Soldiers. *See* black soldiers

business ventures, side, 19, 60, 101–2, 109, 112
butchering animals, 33
button replacing, 44, 60

cabin living quarters, 70. *See also* housing
Calamity Jane, 113
camels, 65
Camp Date Creek, Arizona, 86
camp followers, 18–19, 100, 112–13. *See also* traveling with soldiers
Camp Halleck, Nevada, 116
Camp McDermitt, Nevada, 110
Camp McDowell, Arizona, 60, 68
Camp Town, 67. *See also* housing
Camp Verde, Texas, 65
candles rations, 53
cartoons, *24–25, 41, 52*
cast iron slugs, *42, 44*
Cathay, William. *See* Williams, Cathy
cauldrons, 37, 39
Cavallo, Dr., 114
Cavanaugh, Mrs., 110, 129
chancroid, 114
chemise, 78. *See also* clothing
chickens, 27, 69
childbirth, 12, 26, 32, 76–77, 82, 86
children: childcare, 32, 77, 86, 104; descriptions of, 27; education of, 16, 47, 78–80; health of, 37, 82–83, 93; images of, *75, 123*; labor by, 44, 77; legitimizing process of, 74; social life of, 77, 87. *See also* family life and responsibilities
child's irons, *43, 44*
cholera, 82
chopping firewood, 37–38
Christmas celebrations, 89, 90
Civil War conflicts, 45, 48–51, 118
class distinctions, 30, 71, 73, 85–89
Cloonan, Bridget, *81, 129*

clothing: drying descriptions for, 40–44; secret code using, 51; sewing responsibilities, 44, 60, 77, 107; styles and fabrics of, 33, 34, 39, 77–78; washing descriptions for, 39–40
coffee rations, 23
cohabitation, 63, 73, 76
congressional recognition of laundresses, 20, 53, 121–24
Continental Army laundresses, 16, 19–20, 33. *See also* laundresses
contraband soldiers. *See* black soldiers
contraceptives, 76
Cook, George, 113
cooking: duties of, 17, 26, 48, 58; methods for, 54, 56–57
coppers, 37, 39
Corbusier, Fanny Dunbar, 86
Corinth Contraband Camp, Mississippi, *31*
cornmeal rations, 53, 58
corsets, 78
cotton clothing. *See* clothing
cows, 60, 63, 103
Coyle, Ellen, 23, 129
crime and punishment, 109–13
Crisp, Sarah, 23, 129
cross-identification, 88, 108–9, 118
Custer, Elizabeth Bacon, 12, 52, 70, 76, 86, 107
Custer, George Armstrong, 57, 110

Dabney, Mrs., 50–51, 129
dancing, 87–91
Daughters of the Regiment, 19
desertion, 20–21, 107, 111
diet, 17, 23, 48, 53–58, 63–64
diphtheria, 68, 82
discharged laundresses, 21, 22, 98, 109, 116, 118. *See also* drumming off the post
discharged soldiers, 98, *117*

diseases, 54–56, 68, 82, 112, 114.
See also health hazards
divorce, 16, 107
doctors. See surgeons
Dodge, R. I., 122
dog licensing, 80
dolly sticks, 39
donkeys, 61
drowning, 35–37
drumming off the post, 11, 20, 110.
See also discharged laundresses
drying clothes job description, 40–44
dugout living quarters, 67, 68, 91.
See also housing
dwellings. See housing
dysentery, 82, 116

education, 13, 16, 47, 78–80. See
also literacy and illiteracy
Eichler, Margaret, 60, 130
entrepreneurial ventures, 19, 60,
101–2, 109, 112
ethnic diversity of laundresses, 22–
23, 26, 107. See also black
laundresses

fabric. See clothing
family life and responsibilities, 73–83,
75, 122, 123. See also children
fashion, 77–78, 87
fat rendering, 33, 34, 58
Fetterman Battle, 64
Field, Charles, 73
fighting and laundresses, 109–11,
114–15
firewood chopping, 37–38
Fitsgerald, (Black) Susan, 63–65, 131
FitzGerald, Emily McCorkle, 30–
32, 85
Fitzgerald, Mrs. Mary A., 131
flag bearers, 19
flat irons, 31, 42–43, 45
Fleming, George, 19–20

Flood, Maggie, 13, 15–17, 17, 131
flour rations, 23, 53–54, 57–58
food, 17, 23, 48, 53–58, 63–64
Ford, James, 93
Ford, John, 102
Forsyth, George, 26
Fort Abraham Lincoln, North
Dakota, 54, 56, 65, 70, 108
Fort Atkinson, Nebraska, 69, 109
Fort Bascom, New Mexico, 110
Fort Brown, Texas, 100, 113
Fort Buford, North Dakota, 54, 56,
67, 77, 112, 124
Fort C. F. Smith, Montana, 57, 111
Fort Coeur d'Alene, Idaho, 90
Fort Concho, Texas, 116
Fort Custer, Montana, 88
Fort D. A. Russell, Wyoming, 15,
22, 74, 76, 91
Fort Davis, Texas, 112
Fort Dodge, Kansas, 68, 80, 104
Fort Garland, Colorado, 93
Fort Harker, Kansas, 56, 70, 80, 91
Fort Hays, Kansas, 60, 82
Fort Keogh, Montana, 67, 68, 111
Fort Lapwai, Idaho, 85–86
Fort Laramie, Wyoming, 66; food at,
54, 56, 60; laundresses of, 15,
16, 23; living conditions of, 34–
37, 63, 70; schooling at, 78–80;
social life at, 87, 88, 110
Fort Larned, Kansas, 74
Fort Leavenworth, Kansas, 90, 94
Fort Mason, Texas, 73
Fort McPherson, Nebraska, 29, 114
Fort Meade, South Dakota, 70, 107,
124
Fort Phil Kearny, 57, 63-64
Fort Rae, New Mexico, 119
Fort Riley, Kansas, 89–90, 104
Fort Robinson, Nebraska, 69
Fort Schuyler, New York, 70
Fort Selden, New Mexico, 112

Fort Sidney, Nebraska, 67–68, 116
Fort Sill, Oklahoma, 67
Fort Sisseton, South Dakota, 74
Fort Stockton, Texas, 76, 116
Fort Totten, North Dakota, 23, 87,
    124
Fort Union, New Mexico, *69,* 71,
    81, 93, 114
Fort Yates, North Dakota, 90
Fort Yuma, California, 68, 102
Fourth of July celebrations, 89–90
Francisco, Sylvia, 114, 131
free black laundresses. *See* black
    laundresses
friendships. *See* social life
fruits, 54, 56. *See also* food
fur for clothing, 78

gardening, 54, 56–57
garments. *See* clothing
garters, 78
gender disguise, 88, 108–9, 118
Gratz, Kate, 104, 132
Great Northern. *See* Bourgette, Sarah
Guernsey, John F., 80

half-way ladies, 86–87
Harper's Weekly, 24–25
health hazards: bathing and, 82; of
    children, 37, 82–83, 93; of
    housing, 63, 68–70; of laundry
    work, 35, 37–38, 45; prostitu-
    tion and, 112, 114. *See also*
    diseases
herbal medicine, 82
Heroine of Fort Brown. *See* Bour-
    gette, Sarah
Hess, Emeline, 94–98, 132
Hess, John W., 94–98
hide for clothing, 78
hierarchy, military and social, 30,
    71, 73, 85–89

Hispanic American laundresses, 26.
    See also laundresses
historical record of laundresses, 13,
    20, 26, 48–50, 91, 109
holiday celebrations, 88–90
Hooker, Joseph, 50–51
horses, 61
hospitals and hospital laundresses,
    19, 32, *41, 55,* 58, 82. *See also*
    surgeons
housing, 30, 32, 45, 48, 63, 65–71
Hurlburt, Mrs., 85, 133
hygiene, 80–82

illiteracy and literacy, 13, 47, 64,
    101. *See also* education
income of laundresses: in army hos-
    pitals, 58–59; benefits of, 51–
    52; of black women, 48; first
    official, 53; flat wages *vs.* piece-
    work, 20, 22, 59–61; of Native
    American women, 23; *vs.* sol-
    dier husbands, 12, 15, 30, 52,
    71
Independence Day celebrations, 89–
    90
Indian Wars, 12, 13, 26, 100
"The Influence of Women" *(Harper's
    Weekly),* 24–25
insects, 56, 58, 68, 69
Irish immigration, 23
ironing boards, 45
irons and ironing, *31, 42–43, 44–45*

Jefferson Barracks, Missouri, 70, 118
job descriptions: animal butchering,
    33; chopping firewood, 37–38;
    drying clothes, 40–44; fat ren-
    dering, 33, 34; lye making, 33–
    34; soap making, 33, 34;
    sorting, 34; washing clothes, 39–
    40; water fetching, 34–37, 80

Johnson, Mrs. Albert Sidney, 73

Kelly, Mrs., 91, 133
Kelton, John C., 121, 122
Kimball, Mr., 56
Kitchen, Anna, 133
Klawitter, Mrs. Fred, 54, 133

language, 101
laundresses: about, 11–12; benefits of, 11, 17, 18, 51–61, 122; childcare by, 32, 77, 86, 104; as cooks, 17, 26; decline of position as, 105, 121–25; discharged, 21, 22, 98, 109, 116, 118; education of, 13, 47; ethnic diversity of, 22–23, 26, 107; family life and responsibilities, 73–83, *75*, 122, *123*; first official, 16–17, 19–20, 53; housing for, 30, 32, 45, 48, 63, 65–71; images of, *24–25*; men as, 22, 24–26, 29, 108; as midwives, 12, 26, 30, 82, 107; nicknames of, 19; as nurses, 93; pensions for, 17, 18, 27, 125, 128; practical jokes and, 118; provisions for, 20; rations for, 122; recorded descriptions of, 26–27; registry of, 22, 127–37; rights of, 20–21; secret military code of, 50–51; social hierarchy and, 30, 71, 73, 85–89; soldiers' benefits of marrying a, 52, 71, 73, 122; statistics on, 26, 121–22; stereotypes of, 11, *52*. See also *specific elements of life and work; specific women*
laundry facilities, 16, 29, 32, 37, 58. *See also* housing; supplies
laundry soap powder, *35*
Leahy, Mrs., 86

Lengthy, 29–30
Linty, 29–30
literacy and illiteracy, 13, 47, 101. *See also* education
Litsinger, Margaret, 79, 133
Littlejohn, Margaret, 77, 133
living quarters. *See* housing
log housing, 68. *See also* housing
Loynes, Charles N., 67
lye making, 33–34

Mahoney, Mrs., 104
Marcy, Randolph, 98, 121, 124
marriage: benefits of, 22, 52, 71, 73, 122; cohabitation, 63, 73, 76; divorce, 16, 107; informal-formal process of, 74–75; of officers and laundresses, 16, 30; polygamy, 76, 100–102; *vs.* single women, 22. *See also* social life
measles, 82
meat rations. *See* beef; pigs and pork
medical care services, 82. *See also* hospitals and hospital laundresses; nurses; surgeons
Members of the Regiment (Nacy), 86
men as laundresses, 22, 24–26, 29, 108. *See also* soldiers
mending clothes, 44, 60
Mexican-American War, 13, 61, 96–97
Mexican laundresses, 107, 110
midwives, 12, 26, 30, 82, 107
Molloy, Bridget, *81*
Montgomery, Mrs., 71, 134
Moriarty, Patrick, 114
Morony, Mrs., 134
Mothers of the Regiment, 19
moving laundresses. *See* traveling with the soldiers
mules, 61

Mulford, Ami F., 26
mumps, 82
murder, 111, 112, 119. *See also* assault and laundresses
music, 75, 87, 88

Nacy, Michele, 86
nannies, 32
Nash, Mrs., 13, 107–9, *108,* 134
Nashville, Tennessee, army hospitals, 55
nationalities. *See* ethnic diversity of laundresses
Native Americans: conflicts with, 57, 85–86, 91, 104–5, 119; government rations for, 23; as laundresses, 23
Nez Perce, 85, 104
Nolan, Nicholas, 116
nurses and nursing duties, *26,* 45, 48, 93, 107
nutrition, 23, 53–58

O'Brien, Nicholas J., 29
officers *vs.* soldiers' family life, 73–75
Ord, Edward O. C., 105, 123
Osborn(e), Sarah, 16–18, 135

parades, 88
Patten, Mrs., 91, 135
pensions, 17, 18, 27, 125, 128
Pest House, 55
Peters, D. C., 114
pets, 50, 61, 80
petticoats, 78
pie-making, 63–64, 107
pigs and pork, 50, 53, 54
polygamy, 76, 100–102
Potts, Mary, 42, 45
practical jokes, 118
preservation of food, 54–57

prostitution, *55,* 64, 65, 102, 111–14. *See also* sexually transmitted diseases
protests, 60
provisions. *See* rations
punishments, 109–13

quarters. *See* housing

race. *See* black laundresses; black soldiers; ethnic diversity
Ramis, Mrs., 71, 135
rank and hierarchy, 30, 71, 73, 85–89
rape, 114–15
rates, flat wages *vs.* piecework, 20, 22, 59–61. *See also* income of laundresses
rations: of food, 23, 53–58; of laundry supplies, 11, 33, 34, *35,* 45, 53; for Native American families, 23; termination of position and, 121, 124
record keeping. *See* historical record of laundresses
registry of laundresses, 22, 127–37
Reminiscences of My Life in Camp (Taylor), 48
repairing clothes, 44, 60
Revolutionary War conflicts, 16–17, 53
rheumatism, 119
rice rations, 53, 54
rights of laundresses, 20–21
Ringold Barracks, Texas, 67
river hazards, 35–37
Roach, Julia, 111, 135
role-playing at historic forts, 11, *13*
Rozsa, Patience, 22, 135

sad irons, *31, 43,* 45
salt, 40, 53, 54
Sanford, Wilmont, 54

sanitation: bathing and, 80–82; housing and, 63, 68–70
scarlet fever, 82
Schnyder, Julia Gill, 79, 132
schooling, 13, 47, 78–80
scurvy, 54–56
seasonal conditions. See summer conditions; winter conditions
secret code using laundry, 50–51
sewing machines, 77
sewing responsibilities, 44, 60, 77, 107
sexually transmitted diseases, 82, 112, 114. See also prostitution
shawls, 78
single vs. married women, 22
Sioux, 91
slave laundresses. See black laundresses
slave (contraband) soldiers. See black soldiers
slugs (for irons), 42, 44
smallpox, 114
Smith, Mrs. (Sitka, AK), 30–32, 135
smoking, 52
soap, 33, 34, 35, 58
social hierarchy, 30, 71, 73, 85–89
social life, 85–92, 89. See also marriage
sod living quarters, 67, 68. See also housing
soldiers: in black regiments, 21, 23, 47, 118, 123; discharged, 98, 117; education of, 80; garrison regulations for, 21, 114; as laundresses, 22, 24–26, 29, 108; vs. officers' family life, 73–75. See also traveling with the soldiers
sorting job description, 34
spies in Civil War, 50–51
sports, 88
stereotypes of laundresses, 11, 52

stockings, 78
Straw, Maria, 114, 136
strikes by laundresses, 60
Sturgis, Samuel D., 124
Suds Row. See housing; laundresses
sugar rations, 23
summer conditions, 15, 37, 48, 63, 66, 85. See also winter conditions
Summerhayes, Martha, 91, 102–3
supplies: government rations of, 53, 58; for laundry work, 33, 36, 38; soap, 33, 34, 35; tools, 38–39; for traveling laundresses, 98–100. See also laundry facilities; rations
Sullivan, Mary, 103, 136
surgeons: availability of, 82; on laundresses work, 32, 58, 112; on living conditions, 63, 67, 68, 71; opinions of, 56, 76, 114. See also hospitals and hospital laundresses; nurses
sutlers, 19, 33, 112
Sykes, George, 121, 122

Taylor, Susie King, 47–50, 49, 91, 136
teamsters, 31, 94
Ten Eyck, Tenador, 64–65
tent housing, 32, 48, 65–67, 75. See also housing
tetanus, 82
theatrical performances, 88
Thomas, Henry, 121, 122, 124
Tilford, J. G., 112
Tonmichel, Jake, 110
tools, 38–39. See also supplies
transgressions: fighting, 109–11; prostitution, 55, 65, 111–13; stereotypes of, 11, 52
transportation order, 103

traveling with the soldiers: of Bourgette, 19, 100–102; camp followers, 18–19, 100, 112–13; of
Hess family, 94–98; modes of
travel, 103–4; supplies and
wagons for, 98–100, 102–3,
122; transportation orders, *103*;
of Williams family, 93–94
Trobriand, Regis de, 105
troop movement. *See* traveling with
the soldiers
Tubman, Harriet, 50, 136
Tub Town. *See* housing
typhoid, 82

Union Army laundresses, *21, 31,
48, 55*. *See also* laundresses
U. S. Civil War conflicts, 45, 48–51,
64, 118

Van Voast, James, 37
vegetables, 54, 56–57. *See also* food
venereal disease, 82, 112
vermin, 48, 58, 68
vivandière, 18, 19

wages *vs.* piecework rate, 20, 22,
59–61. *See also* income of laundresses
wagonloads, 94
wall tent housing, 32, 48, 65–67,
75. *See also* housing
war hospitals. *See* hospitals and hospital laundresses
War of 1812, 12, 21
wars. See *specific conflicts*
washboards, *36,* 39
washerwomen. *See* laundresses
washing clothes job description, 39–
40
washing dolly, 39
Washington, George, 17, 53

washtubs, 39
waste disposal, 63, 68–69
water fetching, 34–37, 80
weather. *See* summer conditions;
winter conditions
well water, 37
whiskey, 89–90, 109
white clothing, 33, 39, 40. *See also*
clothing
whooping cough, 82
Williams, Cathy, *115,* 116–18, 137
Williams, Ellen, 93, *95,* 137
Williams, John H., 113
Williams, Martha, *115*
wine, 89–90
Winne, Mrs. Charles, 116
winter conditions: food and, 56, 57;
at forts, 15, 37, 70; housing and,
63, 65–67; traveling and, 93–
94; water and, 35, 69; work and,
41. *See also* summer conditions
women: fashion style of, 77–78, 87;
gender disguise, 88, 108–9,
118; illustration of roles of, *24–
25*; as midwives, 12, 26, 30, 82,
107; as nurses, *26,* 45, 48, 93,
107; sewing responsibilities of,
44, 60, 77, 107; single *vs.* married, 22; social life of, 87–92,
89. *See also* laundresses; marriage; *specific women*
wood, 33, 37–38
woolen clothing, 12, 34, 39–40, 78.
See also clothing
wringer, clothes, *38, 41*

Young, Brigham, 98
Young, Mrs. Peter, 20, 137

Acknowledgments

N obody gets where they are going without the help of others, and that is true of the writing of this book. The late Walter Reuland and his wife, Trudy, were instrumental in kindling my interest in army laundresses. I started doing a little research, and eventually it became a passion. My husband, Mark Rehwaldt, never complained when I said I wanted to go to Kansas in the middle of summer to see various forts and historical sites, or to Texas and New Mexico in March for the same purpose, or to Montana . . . (you get the picture). At each stop, I found a little bit more information. Eventually, that information—scribbled on scraps of paper and in spiral notebooks—filled a good-sized box. Meanwhile, Walt and Trudy kept encouraging me to write this book. "Someday," I always replied.

"Someday" became "now" about two years ago. I had a rough draft completed and I pitched it to Nancy Curtis at High Plains Press. With many suggestions and much guidance, I am now sharing my passion and information with readers.

A part of those suggestions and much of the guidance came from two fellow writers in particular, Marjorie Daley and Myra Edwards. Many a night was spent at the local yogurt shop, reading and critiquing this work.

A final thanks to my dear friend Niki DeLancey for continued encouragement and for keeping my young mare exercised when I was doing the final wrap up on this book.

Many other folks contributed to this journey. To those I have mentioned, and those that I missed mentioning, thank you.